1,000,000 Books

are available to read at

www.ForgottenBooks.com

Read online
Download PDF
Purchase in print

ISBN 978-1-330-28810-8
PIBN 10014527

THE STORY OF THE JAPANESE PEOPLE, AND ESPECIALLY OF THEIR EDUCATIONAL DEVELOPMENT

BY

James A. B. Scherer, Ph.D., LL.D.

President of Newberry College

Author of "Japan To-Day," "Four Princes," etc.

PHILADELPHIA AND LONDON

J. B. LIPPINCOTT COMPANY

1905

Published May, 1905

Electrotyped and Printed by
J. B. Lippincott Company, Philadelphia, U. S. A.

PREFACE

THIS book, while complete in itself, is also designed as a companion of "Japan To-Day." The other work was intended to be a random portfolio of views, showing contemporary life in Japan under every ordinary condition, and from every attainable angle. The present volume attempts to tell the unified story of the nation in the simplest possible manner. Occasionally, in order to make this book complete, it was necessary to recall matters contained in the other, especially in the opening pages.

The plan of my undertaking is twofold: to tell the bare outline story of the people of Japan, and to give a somewhat more detailed account of their remarkable educational development. The first part of each of the three "books" traces the evolution of the nation, while the remainder tries to show the groundwork from which that process has proceeded.

The period of early national culture extends from the first dim traditions of history to the introduction of Chinese civilization in the sixth Christian century, when Japan put off her swaddling-clothes. The period of adolescence traces the growth of the people under the influence of Chinese culture until that was discarded for Western civilization in the middle of the nineteenth century. "School-days" denotes the progress made under this Occidental tutorship. The whole book is built on the theory that Japan stands to-day at the threshold of a new national manhood: YOUNG JAPAN. The three sub-titles as applied to individual development hardly need an explanation.

Throughout five years the writer was closely associated with Japanese youth, on Japanese soil, and during four of these years was teacher in a government school. That experience supplied the chief material for this book. But I acknowledge grateful obligation to other writers, especially the following:

B. H. Chamberlain, *Things Japanese*, etc.; W. E. Griffis, *The Mikado's Empire*, etc.; David Murray, *The Story of Japan;* F. L. Hawks, *Perry's Expedition;* J. J. Rein, *Japan;* A. B. Mitford, *Tales of Old Japan;*

Lafcadio Hearn, *Japan,* etc.; Robert E. Lewis, *The Educational Conquest of the Far East.*

For recent educational information I thank the Japanese Legation at Washington (especially Mr. Eki Hioki), and also my friend Dr. Julius D. Dreher. But my work could not have been completed without the files of the *Japan Weekly Mail.* Other acknowledgment is made in the text.

A note on the *pronunciation of Japanese proper names* may not be amiss. In the first place, a word may be easily divided into its component syllables by simply applying the rule that wherever a vowel or the diphthong *ai* occurs, there is the end of a syllable; for every syllable in the Japanese language ends either in one of these or with the consonant *n*. Wherever this letter occurs, it is attached to the preceding vowel before the syllable is formed. For example, the name of the greatest Japanese in all history, Iyeyasu, should be hyphenated thus: I-ye-ya-su; and the name of the chief anthology of the native poetry becomes Man-yō-shū.

The marks above this *o* and *u* indicate that the vowel sounds are prolonged, having the

value of *o* in "whole" and of *u* in "rude."
When the vowels are not so marked, they
have the following approximate values:

a as in ah.
e " " men.
i " " machine.
o " " so.
u " " bush.
$ai = I.$

Thus Iyeyasu becomes (phonetically) Ee-
yeh-yah-suh, and Manyōshū is pronounced
Mahn-yoe-shoo, while Hokusai, the greatest
of Japanese artists, is called Ho-ku-sye.
Roughly speaking, there is no accent, all of
the syllables receiving equal emphasis, except when otherwise indicated by the marks
above the protracted vowels.

The book is offered as an humble but honest
attempt to assist in the interpretation of
these marvellous children of the East to their
modern schoolmasters here in the West.

JAMES A. B. SCHERER.

NEWBERRY COLLEGE, S. C.

CONTENTS

BOOK I

EARLY CULTURE

BOOK II

ADOLESCENCE

BOOK III

MODERN SCHOOL-DAYS

ILLUSTRATIONS

BOOK I

EARLY CULTURE

YOUNG JAPAN

EARLY CULTURE

PART FIRST

THE French have a proverb which tells us that "the heart makes the age." And is it not true? Do not all of us know some white-haired woman whose face is alight with the glory of an everlasting youth? That is because there are no wrinkles in her heart. She has kept it young, and it has kept her young.

After the same fashion it is right to speak of "Young Japan." Possessed of an antiquity that loses itself in the mists of primitive tradition, the nation is yet young, because somehow the heart of the people is young. Japan is the most youthful spot on earth. Nowhere else in all the world do the hoary-haired go frequently a-maying; nowhere else do grown-up folk keep eternal holiday, even while they labor; nowhere else, in short, can one find such an overgrown playground. The country itself is a continent done in dainty miniature,—gigantic mountains so crowded for room that their feet are laved by the ocean, tiny Niagaras roaring in constrained cascades, and thousands of toy islets thrown in frolicsome confusion, like so many doll-houses, into the rollicking sea. The commonest vehicle is a grown-up baby-carriage, the far-famed *jinrikisha*, or "pull-man-car;" while the little railway trains and coastwise steamers are of a size to their surroundings. Laughter greets one everywhere, and sparkling eyes, and fun,—provided always that we do not look beneath the surface.

Geologically speaking, Japan is possibly one of the youngest of countries, thrown up by volcanic action from the fathomless depths of the sea. Some of the deepest ocean beds on the surface of the globe are found sheer off her precipitous eastern coasts, indicating terrific disturbances in times of old, while earthquakes of greater or less severity are of daily occurrence now. Active volcanoes are frequent in the mountain range that runs like a backbone down the narrow crescent of islands, and there are many places where the surface of the earth is so cracked and sulphurous that the people call them "Hells." There are four large islands (Hondo, Kyūshū, Shikoku,

Physiography.

and Yezo), and about four thousand smaller
ones, all told; aggregating a total area of a
hundred and fifty thousand square miles, of
which only one-twelfth is arable. That is to
say, the size of the empire (exclusive of col-
onies) is considerably less than the State of
California, with farming lands that could be
embraced almost within the boundaries of
Maryland. The climate varies from frigid to
subtropical, according to the latitude; for
the tenuous chain of islands is over a thousand miles in length. But the entire north-
western coast is notable for its bleakness,
owing largely to the absence of that Pacific
"gulf-stream" which warms the eastern
shores, and thus draws the burden of population in that direction. The arable land
is in a very high state of cultivation, producing opulent crops of rice, tea, barley, mil-
let, and beans, with smaller quantities of such
staples as cotton and tobacco. Mines of coal,
copper, antimony, and iron, with a little silver
and gold, are found in certain localities, and
the entire surrounding ocean is a veritable
Golconda of valuable fishes, from the sperm-
whale to the trout and oyster. The flora of
the country, especially in the south, is so rich
that Japan has often been called a land of

flowers, although the blossoms lack fragrance as the fruits lack flavor. The fauna, however, is somewhat meagre except in northernmost Yezo, which is a different geological type. In the year 1879 Japan became possessed of the Loochoo Islands, lying away to the south; and as a result of the war with China fifteen years later acquired Formosa, not far north of the Philippines, so that Japan is our nearest Eastern neighbor.

Ancient Japan was peopled with an interesting race of bearded hunters, the Ainu, who have been driven by their conquerors farther and farther north until now the pitiful remnant of this vanishing race finds an unsteady foothold in remote Yezo, retaining their primitive habits of life, but cursed, like the American Indian, with the liquors that poison the streams of civilization in Orient and Occident alike. The Japanese are assuredly Mongolians, but of a distinct type from their neighbors in China. Rather are they kin to the Tatar rulers of China, who in the thirteenth century overran the Chinese Empire and have possessed it ever since. Ages ago these Japanese vikings sailed in their Tatar junks to the island home of the Ainu, which they promptly seized

Ethnology.

and eventually called "Nihon," the "land of the rising sun." Our own word "Japan" is a distortion of this native name, coming to us through the Chinese, who told Marco Polo, in the thirteenth century, the first news that Europe had of "Japan."

It is probable that the first settlements were made in the South, by means of two main streams of immigration pouring in by way of Korea. Dr. Baelz, who is the highest authority on this subject, believes that these two separate currents of settlement account for the two divergent types that prevail in Japan at present. Among the lower classes, who possibly represent the earlier immigration, one finds a somewhat swarthy complexion, a compact—almost stunted—figure, and powerful development of limb. "Clearer, yellowish-white complexion, a slenderer figure, more symmetry in all parts of the body, and a slighter development of limb, are notable characteristics of the second type," dominant among the aristocracy. Between these two distinct extremes there exist a number of varieties, but all agree in being plainly Mongolian. The reader may dismiss as unworthy of serious attention those sensational journalistic "stories" that identify the

Japanese with the lost tribes of Israel or even class them as negroid. On the other hand, he should distinguish them clearly from the Chinese. Besides marked physical differences, the two races are spiritually diverse. The fundamental distinction is that between esthetics and ethics. The Japanese cares everything for beauty, the Chinaman cares very little for it. But the Chinese are universally allowed to be far more trustworthy. There are bankers of prolonged experience in the East who have never known of a defaulting Chinaman; but woful are their tales of Japan! The key-note to the Japanese character is sentimentalism; that of the Chinese is conservatism. It is the difference between the Gaul and the Teuton.

The distinction between the Japanese and the Chinese is nowhere seen more clearly than in language study. Japanese

Language.

is a language totally unlike the other, belonging to the Ural-Altaic group, with strong affinities for Korean. In the course of time, however, proximity had its effects, and the enterprising islanders received from China enormous linguistic donations that have lain on the surface of Japanese ever since as cream on the surface of milk. Chinese is infinitely richer, and holds itself above the scant elementary speech with a certain aristocratic aloofness that can always be easily distinguished. This habit of borrowing from others, indeed, has always marked Japan as one of the strongest of national characteristics, strikingly exemplified recently by the wholesale appropriation of European civilization, in place of the worn-out Oriental garb supplied by munificent China for so many hundreds of years. Japan, deficient in original genius, has wonderful powers of receptivity and adaptiveness. She has been a sort of eclectic among the nations, choosing the best that they had to bestow, and giving it an ingenious and distinctive twist that makes it essentially "Japanese." This is true in art, letters, science, military equipment, and everything else that has made up the civilization of the country both past and present. Unoriginative Japan is an imitative genius.

But let us hark back to the babyhood of the race. Japanese mythology does not for a moment agree with the prosaic account that has just been given of the way that Japan came to be. It teaches that the beautiful islands were made by the

A Myth with a Moral.

gods themselves, two of whom came down to
live there, becoming the progenitors of the
present inhabitants, who are thus the true
"sons of heaven." The advent story of
those divine progenitors is certainly interesting, and is suggestive of many things.
Izanagi, the god, and Izanami, the goddess,
each took a walk around the borders of the
newly created realm, going in opposite directions. At length they met. Instantly Izanami exclaimed, "Oh, what a beautiful
man!" But Izanagi was displeased that a
woman should precede him in anything, even
in the matter of flattering speech; so this
literal lord of creation commanded that they
walk around the island again and that the
goddess keep silent upon their meeting, thus
giving him his divine right of precedence.
Izanami meekly obeyed him, and when next
they met, she held her nimble tongue, while
her liege lord sluggishly ejaculated, "Oh,
what a beautiful woman!" *

* Mr. Hearn summarizes the native cosmogony as follows: In the beginning neither force nor form was manifest; and the world was a shapeless mass that floated
like a jelly-fish upon water. Then, in some way, earth
and heaven became separated; dim gods appeared and
disappeared; and at last there came into existence a

This story is unintentionally suggestive of several important conclusions, which are in perfect accord with the facts. The Japanese woman is brighter by nature than the average Japanese man. But the man, by the use of brute force, compels her to give way before him, then speaks the woman's speech after her. So Eve has her way after all. Japan has practised for ages the subjection of woman. But there, as elsewhere, the truth is that "the hand that rocks the cradle rules the world!"

Reliable Japanese history does not begin until during the fifth century of the Christian era, although native tradition fixes the founding of the empire in the year 600 B.C. According to this tradition, the father of his country was the first emperor, Jimmu, evidently a descendant of

Legendary History: Jimmu.

male and a female deity, who gave birth and shape to things. By this pair, Izanagi and Izanami, were produced the islands of Japan, and the generations of the gods, and the deities of the Sun and Moon. The descendants of these creating deities, and of the gods whom they brought into being, were the 8000 (or 80,000) myriads of gods worshipped by Shintō. Some went to dwell in the blue Plain of High Heaven; others remained on earth and became the ancestors of the Japanese race.

those Tatar tribes that had secured a foot-hold in the southernmost island of Kyūshū. At the head of a host of his kinsmen, Jimmu at length crossed the Inland Sea into the main island of Hondo, and his migratory hordes, as their numbers increased, pushed steadily on towards the north. Their progress was disputed by the Ainu, but the fresh race was invariably victorious. It appears, also, that tribes of pygmies were encountered, contemptuously called ''earth-spiders,'' because their homes were but holes in the ground. Traces of these primitive pit-dwellers are still to be found in Yezo, where they were long ago exterminated by the Ainu, when driven thither by their own conquerors, the Japanese. The victorious Jimmu is said to have built for himself a palace in the province of Yamato, and from this circumstance ''Yamato'' is a name sometimes employed, and especially in poetry, to denote the whole empire of Japan.

Yamato-dake, ''the bravest in Yamato,'' is the name of a great legendary hero, the **Yamato-dake.** younger son of the twelfth emperor according to the traditional line. The first incident recorded of his romantic career shows that at an early day the principle of filialism had been inculcated as a fundamental virtue in the consciousness of worthy Japanese. Yamato-dake had a sluggish elder brother, who was negligent in his attendance on his father's imperial banquets. The Emperor told Yamato-dake to teach the older son his duty. Upon being asked, a few days later, whether his brother had been reproved, Yamato-dake coolly answered that he had even slain him and thrown his carcass to the dogs! Such was the contempt which this early Japanese hero, the idol of modern Japanese youth, felt for a man, albeit his brother, who might be deficient in filialism.

Another proof that this great tenet of Confucian ethics found early development in Japan lies in the fact that when, in primitive days, the death of a prince occurred, all his retainers were buried alive around him where he lay. For filial piety in Japan and China is not limited to one's parents by any means. The doctrine is extended to all who are in authority, the obligation becoming the more intense as the authority ascends, so that, at the last, supreme allegiance is due the Emperor as the veritable "Son of heaven."

It is doubtless owing to this great principle of Japanese "morality" that suicide came early to be regarded as a virtue. When a subject could do nothing else for his superior, he at least could die for him, and many are the deified heroes of *hara-kiri*, or "bowel-piercing," this being in Oriental usage the substitute for throat-cutting in the West.

These ancient ideals, which seem to us so utterly unideal, are still warmly cherished Japanese by the patriotic youth of Japan, who Chivalry. boast that *Yamato-damashii*, or the "Japanese spirit," is unique, supreme, among all the knightliness that the world has known. It is a striking illustration of the spiritual diversity of mankind to know that a bright and alert race, who have adopted our manners without adopting our morals, can cherish a "chivalry" which scorns womanhood and a "courage" that commends the cowardice of self-destruction. But it is even so. When I assigned to a class of Japanese youth, towards the close of the war with China, an essay on "The Noblest Deed I ever Heard of," nine out of ten of them selected the suicide of the Chinese admiral to illustrate the point in question. Ting, when compelled to surrender, had committed suicide out of a sense of fealty to his master the Emperor of China; and this, forsooth, was the noblest deed of which they had ever heard!

Another quality commended of the Japanese is that of "foxiness." The fox, indeed, is a sacred animal, whose image appears at the door of many a temple, and whose spirit is accredited with *The Prince and the Outlaws.* supernatural powers in possessing the spirit of men. Chief among the heroic exploits of Yamato-dake, who had such large store of *Yamato-damashii,* was the following. His father, struck with the boldness he had shown in the slaying of his brother, sent the young prince south to employ his wits and weapons against two notorious outlaws. The prince, who was slender in figure and of a delicate beàuty, clothed himself in feminine garments, and, with a sword concealed beneath his robes, danced so bewitchingly before the two brothers that they invited the fair danseuse into their private tent. There, when they were quite unarmed, he drew his weapon and ferociously slew the elder outlaw, the other attempting to escape. But Yamato-dake thrust him through the back with his already bloody sword, and would have withdrawn it to complete the slaying, had not the outlaw begged him to withhold an instant until he could ask a single question.

"Who art thou?" he wonderingly inquired; and Yamato-dake told him.

The dying outlaw, when he heard the name, said that hitherto there had been none so brave as he and his elder brother, "but henceforth thou shalt be praised as the bravest in Yamato!"

Then this gentle legend tells us that the prince drew forth his sword and "ripped open the outlaw as it were a ripe melon!"

The prince spent his life in the whole-souled service of his father the Emperor, dying at last while on a military expedition, in the thirty-second year of his age, saying that his only regret in dying was that he could no longer serve the Emperor.

Notwithstanding the Japanese scorn for women, one of the greatest figures in Japan-
A Japanese ese legend is that of the Empress
Amazon. Jingō. It was she who, despising her feeble consort, proposed and actually conducted a victorious invasion of Korea. The traditional date of this important event is fixed in the year 200 A.D. The Japanese have never quite yielded the claim to Korea which

AN ANCIENT JAPANESE AMAZON.

they once based on this alleged Amazonian incursion.

But the chief importance of that ancient invasion lay in the fact that by this means Japan, hitherto isolated, now established relations with the Asiatic continent. *First Contact with China.* From this period dates the beginning of those Chinese influences that have been of such enormous consequence in the development of the Japanese people. The chief of these early influences was the importation of letters, which is alleged to have occurred in the year 284 A.D. Previous to this time the Japanese were without means of recording historical events. It is significant that from this time forward the alleged ages of the emperors suddenly drop from incredible longevity to the normal span of human life, indicating that figures, which "never lie," now begin to take the place of fancy.

Up to the period of continental contact the conditions of Japanese life seem to have been simple in the extreme. Animal food was used much more freely *Early Japanese Culture.* than has been the case since the coming of Buddhism. Tea, which is now so extensively cultivated, seems then to have been unknown.

Agriculture, in fact, was of the crudest and most primitive type. The dwellings were frail oblong huts, their framework of sapling logs being held together by twisted vines. Travel was chiefly on foot, no wheeled vehicles being in use. The implements of warfare were spears, bows and arrows, and swords. Clothing was made from the bark of the mulberry-tree, now used in the manufacture of paper. But when China was once tapped, and the rich wine of her ancient civilization began to filter slowly into Japan, the fluid culture of the Asiatic continent became strangely refined and rarefied by its absorption into this fresh environment. The Japanese people, as has been already remarked, have the gift of daintily individualizing all that they get from abroad, and of somehow refining it, so that a peony becomes a rose. This, doubtless, is due to their marvellous esthetic gifts, in respect of which they are chief among the nations of the world.

Esthetics and ancestor-worship are the foundation stones of the native religion of Japan,—Shintō, "the way of the gods." Morality, as we understand the word, has nothing to do with Shintō. Native writers, indeed, have denied that the

Religion: Shintō.

Japanese have any need for moral guidance. "In Japan there is no necessity for any system of morals, as every Japanese acts aright if he only consults his own heart,"—on the other hand, "morals were invented by the Chinese because they were an immoral people;" these are the literal words of one of the greatest disciples of Shintō. Ancestor-worship is the great, the sole commandment of the law. But the esthetic tastes of the people prompt them to the poetical expression of this worship. Therefore the chosen sacred places are spots of great natural beauty,— these shrewd folk realizing that nature builds more noble monuments than man. Every wooded dell and silvery cascade, each limpid lake and lofty hill, is consecrated by a shrine to the memory of the reverend dead. Far from morality—as we understand it—inhering in the Japanese conception of religion, phallicism was until recently an integral part of Shintō.

Buddhism was imported from China, by way of Korea, about the middle of the sixth century of the Christian era. With their customary intellectual hospitality, the Japanese accepted it with open arms. And with remarkable plasticity,

Buddhism.

Buddhism moulded itself towards the encompassment of Shintō, so that now the two cults are often inextricably interwoven, though the Shintō share of the woof is sometimes exceedingly small. In the seventeenth century, Shintō made an effort to recover its independence, and even now, for obvious political purposes, is the recognized "religion" of the state, since it teaches the divinity of royalty. But Buddhism, the great religion of India, is enormously more attractive of actual devotion than the childish Shintō, and wields a powerful sway over the ignorant masses of the Japanese people to-day. It deifies the forces of nature into innumerable gods, but does not teach the doctrine of a personal God. It believes in the perpetuation of existence through innumerable and ever-varying forms, but teaches that our highest goal is non-existence. It derives its greatest strength from the immortal personality of its illustrious founder, but minimizes the idea of personality in ourselves. Its motto is knowledge, but its Japanese devotees are confined to the ignorant masses. Yet it undoubtedly did much for Japan. "All education was for centuries in Buddhist hands. Buddhism introduced art, introduced medicine, moulded the folk-lore of the country, created its dramatic poetry, deeply influenced politics and every sphere of social and intellectual activity. In a word, Buddhism was the teacher under whose instruction the Japanese nation grew up." But Buddhism is fallen from its high estate as a teacher. The intelligent classes now treat religion with contemptuous indifference, or affect the unmixed "morality" of Confucius.

Confucianism is not a religion at all. It is a cold and heartless system of "morals." Coming to Japan at a very early day with other great intellectual importations from China, it long remained pervasively latent. But through the influence of the great Emperor Iyeyasu it began to displace Buddhism as the national preceptor early in the seventeenth century, and still continues to hold a large proportion of the intelligence of Japan in at least a nominal allegiance. Its main tenet is the doctrine of filial piety applied to all the relationships of life. It despises the character of woman, and treats her as worse than a slave.

Confucianism.

As an instance of the emphasis laid on the doctrine of filialism in the training of Japanese children, we may cite the book called the "Four and Twenty Paragons," the

"The Four and Twenty Paragons."

same being the record of two dozen mythical heroes who are held up as models for the emulation of all worthy youth. Of one of these paragons it is told that, although his mother was but a stepmother, and one who treated him very cruelly at that, yet his sense of filial duty was so great that in winter, when the streams were frozen, he would lie naked on the ice, thereby melting a hole with the warmth of his body, so that he might catch fish to satisfy the whims of her appetite. Another would lie unclothed upon the floor at night, without mosquito netting, to entice the bloodthirsty insects from their attempts to pierce the nets of his parents. A third, and a girl this time, threw herself into a tiger's jaws to save her father; while still another paragon, grown to manhood, buried his own child alive in order to have more food to support his aged mother. But the chief of all the paragons, perhaps, was he who, when seventy years of age, wrapped himself in swaddling-clothes and sprawled upon the floor in order to delude his very aged parents into the happy belief that they were still a young married couple, and he their infant son!

In such fashion run the stories of these two dozen marvellous paragons. And such are the chief ideals instilled into the eager minds of the little Japanese children. If we pursue the subject further, we find that the five relationships inculcated by Confucianism are these: obedience to parents, loyalty to masters, concord between husband and wife, harmony among brothers, and a mutual fidelity in our intercourse with others. The Imperial Rescript on Education, promulgated in 1890 and since that time revered as being both holy and inspired, closely follows these traditional outlines of Confucianism. Confucius is certainly merciful to the man whose wife will not live in concord with him, for in his "seven reasons for divorce" he includes, together with jealousy and disobedience to one's mother-in-law, the fault of overmuch talking!

Shintō, Buddhism, and the ethics of Confucius are the three chapters in the religious primer of young Japan; and this triune religious *The Evolution of Racial Ideals.* influence very largely accounts for the Japanese nation to-day. Mr. Lafcadio Hearn, whose last and most notable work is such a startling compound of brilliant truths and glaring misstatements, is undoubtedly correct—from one point of view—in his fundamental assumption that "the history of Japan is really the history of her religion." But this statement may be very misleading. Other thoughtful writers have gone so far as to say that the Japanese have no religious instincts whatever. The difference is simply in the point of view. Mr. Hearn, an ardent disciple of Herbert Spencer, means by religion little more than the folk-lore traditions of a people, crystallized at length into a cult, and modified by changing environment; but the ordinary writer thinks of religion as a comprehensive system of morals. Shintō itself is not so much a cause as a product; not so much an explanation of how the Japanese people came to be what they are morally, as a simple witness of what they were in the beginning. There is no system about it, and it has no positive morals. In other words, Shintō is merely a record of primitive race characteristics: the record of a beauty-loving, ancestor-worshipping, barbaric tribe of men. Its sole moral tenet of filial piety was without doubt derived from Confucius, and there is reason to think that even its animism came from the aboriginal Ainu. It presents an interesting record of the transition of primitive men from ghost-fear to ghost-love and ghost-reverence; it reveals the gradual evolution of the clan idea on the basis of a common ghost-ancestry; but it does not account for anything, because it is not a philosophy, it is only a history. Confucianism accounts for a great deal. It brought to Japan her first formal revelation of moral law. Its commandment to honor the elders seemed a natural expansion of Shintō, bringing the spirit of ancestor-worship down from the realm of ghosts, and making it incarnate in the living. It greatly strength- The Religion of ened the clan idea, because it Patriotism. taught that the clan-leader was to be revered as a father. Confucianism grafted upon Shintō built up the Japanese state. The Emperor, or strongest of the head clansmen, was recognized as supreme father of all, and therefore entitled to supreme duty. But the Shintō cosmogony (see page 22) recognized him as the chief of the divinely descended, who came down from the sun; himself the chief "son of heaven." Confucianism brought to this native conception its positive moral mandate of obedience, concentrating all moral motives in an acme of devotion to this heaven-descended father of his people—and, lo! "a God incarnate, a race-divinity, an Inca descended from the Sun." That is the Japanese emperor. One can thus gain a glimpse of the profound sources of Japanese loyalty. For untold generations all of the moral and religious ideals of this people have centred themselves in their emperor. They have known no other religion than patriotism; their god has been their Mikado. It is little wonder that the government desires the perpetuation of Shintō, and that the official education of the people is based on Confucian principles. What would happen should the people lose faith in their sun-god? Japan is trying a venturesome experience in her attempt to put new wine into old bottles. The all-powerful clans that control her present destinies seek to strengthen these old bottles by fostering the growth of pure Shintō. A result is seen in the fact that the number of Shintō temples is increasing at the rate of more than eight hundred a year; the total number in 1901 being 195,256. Everything is done for the encouragement of Shintō. Imperial priestesses preside at the principal shrines; soldiers and students are required to perform periodical worship at ancestral graves; and Shintō priests alone are officially sent to the front with the army. The protection of innumerable deities is promised to the faithful in every department of life. The carpenter is encouraged to don a priestly costume at a certain stage of his work, perform rites, chant invocations, and place the house under the protection of the gods. The housekeeper is taught to invoke the god of the wells, of the cooking-range, of the cauldron and sauce-pan and rice-pot. The farmer is led to the shrines of the gods of the gardens, of the fields, of the woods, and the hills, and the bridges; there is even a god of the scarecrows! This is really a part of the system of ancestor-worship; for it is long-departed ghosts that have finally become invested with divine honors, until they are known as the *Kami*, the "upper ones," the divinities. But the imperial ancestors are the gods of these gods, as the sun dominates the universe. The highest example of typical Shintō devotion is found in the ancient province of Izumo, where the worshipper, immediately upon rising, performs his morning ablutions; and "after having washed his face and rinsed his mouth, he turns to the sun, claps his hands, and with bowed head reverently utters the simple greeting: 'Hail to Thee this day, August One!' In thus adoring the sun he is also fulfilling his duty as a subject,—paying obcisance to the Imperial Ancestor.'' And that is the meaning of the blood-red sun set at the centre of the Japanese flag: symbol of the sun-descended Emperor.

Shintō, aided by Confucianism, is thus at the heart of the government, and is the key Cleanliness and to the racial ideals. Mr. Hearn Beauty. further tells us that ''the Japanese love of cleanliness—indicated by the universal practice of daily bathing, and by the irreproachable condition of their homes—has been maintained, and was probably initiated, by their religion. Spotless cleanliness being required by the rites of ancestor-worship,— in the temple, in the person of the officiant, and in the home,—this rule of purity was naturally extended by degrees to all the conditions of existence.'' But this again is probably the confusion of effect with cause. The Japanese by nature are a beauty-loving people, true modern Greeks; if cleanliness be next to godliness, it is certainly of the very essence of beauty. Shintō is a mere ritual of existence, the record of the inherent characteristics of a race.

Buddhism, in spite of its philosophical inconsistencies, is a positive force even greater than Confucianism. It has been of incalculable benefit to this irrepressible Culture. Tatar race with its fundamental tenet of self-repression, or self-control; and has greatly modified their native Tatar cruelty with its doctrine of the sacredness of life. But its chief influence has been educational. As we shall see later on, "Buddhism brought the whole of Chinese civilization into Japan, and thereafter patiently modified and reshaped it to Japanese requirements,"—with the assistance of the Japanese themselves. One of the chief historical features of Buddhism is its marvellous power of adaptiveness to environment without loss of its own essential persistency, so that at the last it is likely to adapt its environment to itself,—with benevolent assimilation, let us say. This it accomplished so perfectly in relation to the negative Shintō that the government, when aroused to the political necessity of strengthening the old bottles against the fermentation of the new foreign wine, proceeded to the disestablishment of Buddhism (1871). It **had** usurped the very throne, and had gradually become the state religion. From time to time throughout the following pages we shall see that it had untold influence in the culture of Young Japan.

EARLY CULTURE
PART SECOND

Japanese babies are invariably and invincibly charming, except that their parents, with all of their passion for cleanli- Japanese Babies. ness, strangely enough neglect the facial toilet of their offspring. Nor is it altogether true, as is sometimes said, that Japan is "the children's paradise." If the newcomer happens to be a girl, the father is likely to meet his congratulatory friends with the exclamation, *"Shakkin no tamago!"*—a punning phrase that means "an egg of debt,"—the idea being that a girl baby is only the germ of enormous and useless expense. And, boy or girl, the prac- Infanticide. tice of infanticide is not uncommon. Being restrained by no religious scruples, a poverty-stricken parent will sometimes snuff out the infant life rather than spare it to a future of want and penury. The supreme moral principle of filialism, or the duty of the child to the parent, tends conversely to emphasize in the parent's mind his own su-

preme power over the child. At the behest
of his own filial duty, for example, the father
must sacrifice his paternal duties and affec-
tions absolutely. An instance is on record
where an ignorant peasant was told by an
equally ignorant priest that if he wished his
aged mother's failing eyesight to be restored,
he must feed her a human liver. The peasant was about to sacrifice his child for this
Wife-Murder.   purpose, when his wife interposed
and yielded up her own life, both
to save her little one and to be at the same
time faithful to the behests of "piety." It
was not long after this event that I called
upon the lads in the Japanese school to write
essays on "The Noblest Deed I ever Heard
of." One of them chose this incident for his
theme.

On the whole, however, the lot of the average baby seems to be a very happy one, and
certainly he appears so, playing in the streets
all day, and having almost innumerable festivals planned apparently for his own peculiar delight.

Ceremony attends his advent into the world
Ceremonies of   and accompanies him to the thresh-
Childhood.   old of manhood. Japan, indeed,
is the country where nothing can be done

without ceremony. And this has been the case from immemorial times. The rites that dignify the life of a little Japanese baby to-day are possibly to a great extent identical with those that were performed for Yamato-dake himself. A glimpse into a famous "handbook of etiquette" will be interesting, as illustrating the traditional ceremonial treatment of childhood. Very little ceremony attends the giving of the name, we are told, which takes place when the child is a week old, and is consequently known as "the congratulations of the seventh night." Some honored relative selects and bestows this particular name, which is only temporary, lasting through the period of childhood. Another name is afterwards bestowed for use in the grown-up world. But the bond between the child and his naming-sponsor is a real one, so that if the sponsor should at some time change his own name, as is often done in Japan, the child must take a new one also. The manuals of etiquette further tell us that on the seventy-fifth or hundred and twentieth day after birth, the child leaves off its baby-clothes, or perhaps "long dresses," as we should say; and the event is celebrated as a family holiday. It is also on the hundred and twentieth day that the ceremony of weaning occurs, although the ceremony often far precedes the fact. The child, arrayed in his choicest garments, is brought in and given to the weaning-sponsor: a man in the case of a boy, a woman in the case of a girl. The weaning-sponsor takes a cup of consecrated rice and places it on a little ceremonial table that stands beside him. Then, dipping his chop-sticks three times in the rice, he quietly inserts them in the mouth of the child, pretending thus to feed it. " Five cakes of rice-meal are also placed on the left of the little table, and with these he again pretends to feed the child three times. When this ceremony is over, the child is handed back to its nurse, and three winecups are then produced on a tray. The sponsor drinks three cupfuls, and presents a cup to the child. When the child has been caused to pretend having drunken twice, it receives a present from the sponsor, whereupon it is supposed to take the third drink. Dried fish is then brought in, and the baby, having now drunk thrice, passes the cup, as it were, to the sponsor, who proceeds to do likewise. The drinking is repeated, and the weaning-sponsor then receives a present from the child. A feast should always be prepared, according to the means of the family.''

Doubtless the weaning of the child receives its ceremonial significance from the fact that the child is now supposed to begin its independent existence, being no longer just a part of the mother. This was likewise a custom with the ancient Hebrews, as when one reads of the weaning of Isaac. The Japanese child, however, is sometimes not actually weaned until he is as old as Ishmael was on the occasion of the weaning of Isaac. Now and then you may see great lads of ten years or more taking their nourishment directly from their mothers.

When Kodomo San, or Mr. Baby, reaches the end of his third year, his family may celebrate the festival of letting his hair begin to grow. Hitherto they may have kept him shaven bald, but now he is supposed to have reached an age when he has a right to his hair. A sponsor is selected, as before; and amid elaborate ceremony, including copious drinking of wine, Kodomo San is solemnly invested with hair. The style in which it henceforth grows varies with the taste of the parents. Frequently a circular space is kept mowed smooth on the crown of the head, leaving a bushy encircling tonsure like that of monks. Again, the hair is allowed to grow only in tufts, from the sides and the back of the head, like handles. But there is no limit set to the whimsical mother's taste in this matter of tonsorial landscape gardening.

When Kodomo San is four years old, he is invested with the dignity of breeches. '' On this occasion again a sponsor is called in. The child receives from the sponsor a dress of ceremony, on which are embroidered storks and tortoises,—emblems of longevity; with fir-trees and bamboos, emblematic respectively of steadfastness and uprightness of heart. The child is placed upright on a checker-board, facing the auspicious point of the compass, and invested with the dress of ceremony. He also receives a sham sword and dirk. The usual ceremony of drinking wine is observed.'' Thus another milestone on the road to manhood has been passed.

With these formal ceremonies of childhood, jolly informal festivals are abundantly inter-Festivals of mingled The chief of them are Childhood. the girls' festival in March, and that of the boys in May. The former is called The Feast of Dolls; for on the third of March all the doll-shops in all the cities are decked out in such fashion as to set the little ones fairly agog with delight. The Japanese excel in doll-making. In Western countries we rarely see any but the cheaper grades of their work. But in Japan one may be actually deceived by the marvellous life-likeness of these little men-images, taking them to be real children. Imagine a doll-festival day in Japan! All of the toy shops are filled with tiny models of all sorts of people and things, the whole Japanese world in miniature. It is the day of the girls' rejoicing.

But the country wears its most picturesque aspect during the boys' festival, two months later. The carp is the chosen symbol of boy-hood, because he swims upstream, against all manner of obstacles, resolved at all cost of endeavor to make his own way in the world. So the people make great toy carps of paper, tough and fibrous, with a large hoop at the mouth, and a much smaller hoop at the tail. Then they hoist these great carps to the top of high flag-staffs, one for the roof of each house where boys are; and the wind goes in at the mouth and fills out the sides of the fish to life-like proportions, and they squirm and wriggle and dart through the air for all the world as though the ocean were above us. Doubtless the world does not hold a more picturesque spectacle than Japan affords on the fifth day of every fifth month. Moreover, plenteous bows and arrows and other warlike toys abound in all the shops, so that at this time at least Japan is a true paradise for boys.

Amid an atmosphere of poetry and world-old romance, hedged in by ceremonial and enlivened by frequent festive jollity, taught strange duties compounded of both good and evil, right and wrong, the little master of the East journeys on the way to full-orbed manhood. I can recall him plainly now, as I have seen him many a time: bright-eyed, rosy little tonsured monk, wrapped in his robes of rustling silk, borne on the bending back of a slightly older brother,—I can see him, and I know how to love him, too. For if there is anything in all the world more engaging, more appealing, more heart-searching and compelling than the little baby Jap, with all he stands for and with all he is, it can be only the child we call our own. A touch of nature is said to make the whole world kin; and surely it is this world-wide human nature that informs the following touching lines written and dedicated to his children by a Japanese provincial governor twelve hundred years ago,—

" What use to me the gold and silver hoard?
  What use to me the gems most rich and rare?
  Brighter by far—ay! bright beyond compare—
  The joys my children to my heart afford!"

BOOK II

ADOLESCENCE

ADOLESCENCE

PART FIRST

THE history of the Japanese people has been modified and even moulded by two supreme events, one occurring about the middle of the sixth Christian century and the other in the middle of the nineteenth. These were the importation of Chinese civilization, through Buddhism, and the introduction of Western civilization, with Christianity. These two events consequently determine the divisions of this book. Having already considered the simple beginnings of Japanese life, we shall now concern ourselves with the period of Chinese influence, which tutored Japan's adolescence;" and the final chapter will treat of maturer "school-days" under the tutorship of the nations of the West.

Chinese influences began to filter in, as we have seen, so long ago as the third century, in consequence probably of the Korean invasion under the Empress Jingō. But when Buddhism was imported, three centuries later, these forces poured in like a flood. Korea was again the interme-

Chinese Culture.

diary channel. An ambassador from that country presented the Japanese emperors with images of the founder of Buddhism, Sakya-Muni; with copies of the Buddhist Bible, and even with missionary priests and a nun. The new faith was at first bitterly opposed, however, chiefly on the ground of patriotism,—officers high in the state contending for the native religion of Shintō, resisting even unto blood this missionary enterprise from Korea. But after forty years of struggle for admission, Buddhism gained the ascendency, and the name of Shōtoku Taishi (A.D. 572–622) remains notable as the chief promoter of Japanese Buddhism. This prince, who lived in the reign of the Empress Suiko, was a thorough believer in China. Not only is he famous for religious reform, but also for great literary and political innovations. Through his leadership the literary culture of China became henceforth the culture of his own country, and by him the Chinese ideas of government were made the basis for a new form of government in Japan. Not only so, but new arts and industries were introduced, the calendar greatly improved, and the sciences fostered. In other words, a transformation, almost as complete and rapid as the one we have seen take place in our own day, occurred just thirteen centuries earlier, when this remarkably volatile race first felt the touch of the ancient civilization of China. What Commodore Perry has been to the Japan of to-day was Shōtoku Taishi to the Japan of yesterday. They are her two great openers of gates. One let in the light of the Orient, by whose dim effulgence the childhood of this race was illuminated during thirteen centuries; the other un-barred a passage for the full-orbed wester-ing sun when the eyesight of the people could bear it.

We must look somewhat carefully into the nature of the political changes brought about by the Chinese illumination, in order to un-derstand the development of that peculiar form of government which began with Shō-toku Taishi, reached its climax a thousand years later, and was finally overtoppled by the guns of an American frigate. Until the advent of Chinese influences, the government of Japan had been an imperialism, pure and simple. The Emperor was a real ruler, lead-ing his armies and directing his government himself. "This era was the golden age of imperial power.　He was the true executive of the nation, initiating and carrying out the enterprises of peace or war.''　But the adoption of Chinese methods of government speedily changed all of this.　The essence of The Bureaucracy. the change lies in the Bureau idea. Prince Shōtoku, under the Empress Suiko, secured the establishment of an imperial cabinet, which indeed promised to assist in the duties of rulership, but in fact eventually usurped them.　In imitation of the Chinese custom, eight boards, or bureaus, were established, charged with the administration of war, justice, revenue, education, etiquette; and, in short, all of the functions of government.　Ranks were introduced at the same time, embracing twelve distinctions, which were shortly extended to nineteen, and bestowed not for individual talent, but upon families, for hereditary transmission.　True, the Emperor, sole ''son of heaven,'' remained theoretically absolute, but in the hands of his ambitious ministers, and fondled as he was by an effeminate court, he tended steadily towards a loss of his power, and became in the end a mere puppet.

Abdication was encouraged by the ascetic character of Buddhism, the rulers often retiring into Buddhistic monasteries and becoming "cloistered emperors," while an infant successor ascended the throne. The ministers, taking care to see Abdication. that he also should become a monk as soon as he ceased to be an infant, thus held all the reins of power continually in their hands, and saw to it that "abdication" became shortly an unalterable custom of the state. We have record of one emperor's accession at the age of two, and his abdication two years later. Another was appointed at the age of five, and several at the age of ten. Thus the government became essentially bureaucratic, the Emperor degenerating into a mere signet, so to speak, or credential of the families that controlled him.

The Fujiwara family was the first to gain complete control of the government, which they held for four hundred years The Fujiwara
Clan. (A.D. 670–1050). They were above all a family of courtiers, usurping all of the civil offices, but letting the camp alone. They removed the capital from Nara to Kyōto in A.D. 794.* Under their elegant patronage the

---

* "If the Japanese annals are to be trusted, Japan has had no less than sixty capitals. This is to be traced

court became the centre of a brilliant but effeminate culture,—this period being known to this day as the golden age of Japanese classical literature. Very early in the Fujiwara period were produced the two great works which still remain as our chief sources of early Japanese history,—the *Kojiki*, or "Record of Antiquities," in the year 712, and the *Nihongi*, or "Japanese Chronicles," in the year 720.

The classical period of Japanese literature —synchronous with the Fujiwara regency— The Age of Classic Poetry. deserves consideration somewhat in detail. While the *Kojiki* and the *Nihongi* rank as the earliest literary productions, the minstrel had long preceded the historian, as is proved by the ancient verses in which these books abound. Poetry, indeed, forms the earliest literature of every people, for it is the picture-language of childhood. Prose, the language of exact knowledge, does

---

to the fact that in ancient days there was a superstitious dread of any place in which a person had died. The sons of a dead man built themselves a new house. Hence, too, the successor of a dead Mikado built himself a new capital."—CHAMBERLAIN. Nara was the first permanent capital, being the imperial residence for seventy-five years, and throughout seven reigns.

DEER PARK AT NARA.
The first permanent capital of Japan.

not develop in the literature of a race until knowledge itself has developed. Before pen was ever put to paper in Japan, poetic songs were scattered through this poetic land like the myriad vagrant leaves of autumn.

The first collection of these scattered waifs of song was made about the middle of the eighth century, receiving the ap- "The Myriad propriate title of *Manyōshū*, "The Leaves." Garner of a Myriad Leaves." Many anthologies have since been collected, but the "Myriad Leaves" may be said to present the chief examples of Japanese classical poetry, which has more than once been called the one original product of the Japanese mind. Everything else in their ancient store of culture they borrowed whole from China; everything in this modern era is adopted from the West: only the native poetry remains unchanged and unmixed, the sole pure channel for the expression of the native thought.

Of a piece with the antipodal Japanese mind, it is as unlike Western poetry as poetry well could be. It has neither rhyme nor tone, accent nor quantity, and it even scorns "alliteration's artful aid." The sole essential rule of prosody in the construction of ordinary Japanese poetry is to build each stanza unvaryingly of alternate lines of five and seven syllables each, with an extra line of seven syllables commonly marking the close. The most frequent themes are the beauties of nature, the sweetness of love, and the frailty of human life. Chinese words are rigidly avoided. The poems are usually exceedingly brief, the favorite form of metrical expression containing only thirty-one syllables. A specimen of typical Japanese poetry is found in their miniature "national anthem," which is as follows:

> Kimi ga yo wa,
>   Chi-yo ni yachi-yo ni!—
> Sazareishi no
>   Iwa wo to narite,
>   Koke no musu made!

This may be freely translated,—"May the years of the Prince be ten thousand times ten thousand!—until the pebbles grow into boulders, and until these become covered with moss!"

One striking feature of these Lilliputian odes is their elliptical terseness of style. The *hokku* is a form of verse containing only seventeen syllables, as the following example shows:

Asagao ni
Tsurube torarete,
Morai-mizu!

A literal translation of these words utterly fails to convey the dainty poesy of the original,—"The well-bucket having been seized by a morning-glory,—gift-water!" In order to understand this little poem, one needs to be informed that a poetess, on going one morning to the well, found that a morning-glory had twined itself around the rope; and, rather than disturb the clinging tendrils, she went and begged water of a neighbor.

One of the prettiest customs of Japanese etiquette is to speed a parting guest with kindly wishes fashioned into this ancient classic form of dainty verse. At the *sō-betsu-kwai*, or farewell meeting, friends will arise and chant original verses, which often have a distinctly poetical flavor. Frequently, however, this flavor is utterly lost when the poem is turned into English. An amusing story is told which aptly illustrates this point. A certain elderly Englishwoman had so endeared herself to the Japanese court during her residence at the British legation that the Empress herself deigned to honor her with a poem of parting as the gray-haired lady returned to her Western home. The verse was an exquisite type of its class; but in our matter-of-fact English prose the parting lament became: "Westward the gray goose takes her flight!" Needless to say, the word "goose" has no such unhappy connotation in Japanese as in English, nor does Oriental usage esteem gray hairs as other than a crown of glory; so that, robbed of its awkward Occidental suggestiveness, the verse becomes a pretty conceit, and should doubtless be associated with Bryant's noble lines "To a Waterfowl."

Chief of all the poets of Japan was Hitomaro (with the given name Kaki-no-moto), The Poet Hitomaro. many of whose songs are found among the "Myriad Leaves." He is supposed to have died in the year 737 A.D. He was originally of lowly rank, and legend has built up a pretty myth around his given name, which literally means "under the persimmon-tree." We are told that a warrior, going one day into his garden, found standing in the shade of his favorite fruit-tree a child of more than mortal splendor, who, when asked his name, replied: "Father and mother have I none; but the moon and the winds obey me, and my delight is poesy." The warrior's wife being equally charmed with this little child of the muse, they adopted him into their noble home, commemorating his origin in the name they gave him. The legend also tells us that near the poet's grave there grows a great persimmon-tree whose fruit is pointed and black at the end, resembling a Japanese pen in form and color.

Hitomaro's only rival was his contemporary, Akahito, whose compositions are also preserved in "The Garner of a Myriad Leaves." One of the prettiest songs in Japanese poetry—according to Western canons of taste, at least—is one that he composed when ascending Mount Mikasa, near the ancient capital of Nara. It is here given in Professor Chamberlain's translation:

Akahito.

> Oft in the misty spring
> The vapors roll o'er Mount Mikasa's crest,
>   While, pausing not to rest,
> The birds each morn with plaintive note do sing.

> Like to the mists of spring
> My heart is rent; for, like the song of birds,
>   Still all unanswer'd ring
> The tender accents of my passionate words.

5

I call her ev'ry day
Till daylight fades away;
I call her ev'ry night
Till dawn restores the light;—
But my fond pray'rs are all too weak to bring
My darling back to sight.

In addition to the "Myriad Leaves," one other great anthology has been preserved to "The Old and the New." us from the period of classical poetry. It is called the *Kokin-shū*, or "The Garner of the Old and the New," and was compiled in the year 905, chiefly by the great author Tsurayuki. It contains many thousands of the thirty-one syllable stanzas that have been already described, a pretty example consisting in the following lines on "Spring":

Amid the branches of the silvery bowers
The nightingale doth sing: perchance he knows
That spring hath come, and takes the later snows
For the white petals of the plum's sweet flowers.

In his elegant introduction to the *Kokin-shū*, Tsurayuki became the father of Japanese prose, and remains one of its The Age of Classic Prose: Tsurayuki. most illustrious exemplars. Up to his day, all prose compositions had been written in stilted Chinese. Notwithstanding his connection with the court, he broke with the slavish tendencies of the times, and established a native prose literature. His most famous work is the *Tosa Nikki*, this being a diary (*nikki*) which describes a voyage he once made from his native province of Tosa to the capital city, Kyōto. This is the "best extant embodiment of uncontaminated Japanese speech." It led the way for a large number of excellent prose works, consisting chiefly in *monogatari*, or tales. Perhaps the most famous of these is the "Tale of a Bamboo-Cutter," narrating the adventures

Prose Tales.

of a maiden from the moon who sojourned on the earth for a season. The book is so named because the bamboo-cutter is said to have found the Moon-Maiden ensconced in a section of bamboo, where she lay sparkling like gold. But the prose literature of the Japanese, all things considered, reached its fullest and richest development in the *Genji Mono-gatari*, or "The Tale of Prince Genji," and the *Makura no Sōshi*, or "Pillow Book," both of which were written at the beginning of the eleventh century by two noble ladies of the court. We are told that the Genji romance leads all works in Japanese literature in the fluency and grace of its diction, while the Pillow Book is matchless for general artistic excellence. The quotation from the latter which is here given (in Mr. Aston's translation) is remarkable as a graphic bit of description. The author is Madame Sei Shōnagon, of imperial blood, and for some time a lady-in-waiting to her empress. When her mistress died, in the year 1000, she entered a Buddhist convent, where this remarkable "Pillow Book" was composed. In the following selection she imagines herself back at the palace, watching through the "grated windows" a group of rustic visitors in the yard below:

"What fun to watch the farmers' wives and daughters, arrayed in all their hoarded finery, A Woman and riding in their wagons (made Writer. clean for the occasion), as they come to see the races in the court-yard of the palace! . . . How prim and proper they appear, all unconscious of the shock their dignity will get when the wagon jolts across the huge beam at the bottom of the gate, and knocks their pretty heads together, disarranging their hair, and worse still, mayhap breaking their combs! But that is after all a trifle when compared to their alarm if a horse so much as neighs. On this account the gallants of the court amuse themselves by slyly goading the horses with spear and arrow-point, to make them rear and plunge and frighten the wenches home in fear and trembling. How silly too the men-at-arms appear, their foolish faces painted with dabs here and there upon their swarthy cheeks, like patches of snow left on a hillside from a thaw!"

The contemporary authoress, Madame Murasaki, gives sage advice to her sex in the Romance of Prince Genji:

"Women there are," she informs us, "who are too self-confident and obtrusive. These, if they do but discover some slight inconsistency in men, fiercely betray their indignation and behave with arrogance. A man may show a little inconsistency occasionally, but still his affection may remain; then matters will in time become right again, and they will pass their lives happily together. If therefore the woman cannot show a tolerable amount of patience, this will but add to her unhappiness. She should, above all things, strive not to give way to excitement; and when she experiences any unpleasantness, she should speak of it frankly, but with moderation. And if there should be anything worse than unpleasantness, she

A Woman's Opinion of Women.

should even then complain of it in such a way as not to irritate the man. If she guides her conduct on principles such as these, even her very words, her very demeanor, may in all probability increase his sympathy and consideration for her.''

The Fujiwara and the Tokugawa periods alone were anywise notable in literature. That is to say, from the twelfth to the seventeenth century one finds a prolonged barren period, and that for a very good reason: war is not conducive to letters. The Fujiwara and the Tokugawa regencies were eras of peace; therefore they were eras of literature. The Decline of Letters. With the rise of the military power letters decayed, but we shall witness a classic revival under Iyeyasu, the greatest of the Shōguns. If we except the so-called ''Dance Songs,'' only two notable productions saw the light in the prolonged intervening period: the *Hōjōki*, or ''Hermit's Diary,'' written about the year 1200 by a disappointed Buddhist monk; and the *Tsure-zure-Gusa*, or ''Weeds of Idleness,'' composed by another monk a century and a half later. This latter work is really important, especially because of its happy adaptation of Chinese words to the forms of the native language, thus welding the two tongues into a union that makes the speech of modern Japan. The author was Yoshida Kenkō, and he composed his volume of short essays about the year 1345.

Allusion has been made to the "Dance Songs" (*Nō no Utai*) as a product of the otherwise barren age of Japanese literature. The Japanese dance is of ancient religious origin, and is really a series of very slow and very graceful posings. Anciently these movements were executed to the accompaniment of rude choric songs, but early in the fifteenth century certain highly cultivated Buddhist priests developed the *Nō* into a veritable drama, which bore a striking resemblance to the drama of the an- The Ancient cient Greeks. Professor Chamber- Drama. lain informs us that "there was the same chorus, the same stately demeanor of the actors, who were often masked; there was the same sitting in the open air, there was the same quasi-religious strain pervading the whole." In his opinion, some of these lyrical dramas—all of which are anonymous —rank with the cleverest productions of the prolific Japanese pen. His able work on "The Classical Poetry of the Japanese" con-

tains several interesting specimens, of which
the most beautiful is entitled "The Robe of
Feathers." A fisherman, landing on the pine-
clad shore near the base of the peerless
Mount Fuji, hears strains of heavenly music,
while a more than earthly fragrance fills the
air.   Looking in wonder about him, he dis-
cerns a beauteous robe of iridescent feathers suspended from the branches of a pine-
tree.   Seizing it in his hands, he is about to
carry the priceless treasure home with him,
when a lovely Moon-Fairy appears to claim
it as her own.   But the fisherman denies her,
and despair fills her breast because without
her robe of feathers she can never go soar-
ing through the realms of air,—nevermore
return to her celestial home.   At length, however, the fisherman promises to restore the
robe if then and there the Moon-Maiden shall
dance for him one of those far-famed fairy
dances that gladden the hearts of the thirty
happy kings in the palace of the silvery moon.
Rejoiced, the maiden dons her rainbow robe,
and not only dances, but

" The fairy sings, and from the cloudy spheres,
Chiming in unison, the angels' lutes,
Tabrets, and cymbals, and sweet silv'ry flutes,
Ring through the heav'n that glows with purple hues."

LITTLE MAIDENS OF THE SACRED DANCE.

At the last the ravished chorus shouts:

" Dance on, sweet maiden, through the happy hours!
Dance on, sweet maiden, while the magic flow'rs
Crowning thy tresses flutter in the wind
Rais'd by thy waving pinions intertwin'd!
Dance on! for ne'er to mortal dance 'tis giv'n
To vie with that sweet dance thou bring'st from heav'n:
And when, cloud-soaring, thou shalt all too soon
Homeward return to the full-shining moon,
Then hear our pray'rs, and from thy bounteous hand
Pour sev'nfold treasures on our happy land;
Bless every coast, refresh each panting field,
That earth may still her proper increase yield!
      But, ah! the hour, the hour of parting rings!
Caught by the breeze, the fairy's magic wings
Heav'nward do bear her from the pine-clad shore,
Past Uki-shima's widely-stretching moor,
Past Ashi-daka's heights, and where are spread
Th' eternal snows on Fuji-yama's head,—
Higher and higher to the azure skies,
Till wand'ring vapors hide her from our eyes!"

The indifference of the literary Fujiwara clan to the affairs of the camp proved to be the means of their undoing. They had been quite content to leave all of the military glory of the empire to those dominant martial families, the Taira and the Minamoto, while they themselves monopolized the statecraft. This was well

Taira and Minamoto Clans.

enough so long as the Taira and the Mina-moto were subduing rebellions in the fre-quently turbulent provinces; but the time came when there were no longer any rebel-lions to subdue, and the two aggressive clans straightway acquired a fondness for dallying with the statecraft also. The result was a foregone conclusion. The Fujiwara family, enfeebled by the same effeminate environ-ment with which they had surrounded the Emperor, succumbed to these militant ag-gressors; and to the Bureaucratic govern-ment was consequently added the important feature of Militarism.

It was militarism in deadly earnest from the first. For the two great clans, who had

Feudalism.

fought side by side in unity against a common foe, now took to fight-ing each other. The prize of their warfare was the person of the Emperor; even as with the queen of a hive of bees, so in ancient Japanese society the possession of the im-perial person meant to hold the sceptre of the whole situation. The vast forces of the two conflicting hosts were so evenly balanced that their strife lasted more than a century (A.D. 1050–1185). Its most important effect on the development of Japanese history was that it made Feudalism a permanent national institution. "Japan was now converted into a camp; her institutions were feudalized. The real master of the empire was he who, strongest with his sword and bow, and heading the most numerous host, could partition out the land among the chief barons, his retainers." For a hundred years and more the issue of the struggle was uncertain. Then the war ended in the triumph of the Minamoto family; but for seven hundred years after its close its effects were all-powerful in Japanese history through the dominance of that principle of militarism in government which this war had so firmly established. In short, the significance of this great civil war consists in the addition to a bureaucratic government of the military power, and the sum of these two factors is Feudalism.

The Minamoto won their final victory under the leadership of two valorous brothers. The younger of these, Yoshitsune Yoshitsune. by name, has been called the Bayard of Japan. Son of a great Minamoto chieftain, he was left fatherless at a very tender age,—one of the most popular of modern Japanese pictures representing Yoshitsune as a babe in arms, his outcast mother trudging through the pitiless snow, followed by his elder brother and another child, seeking in vain for safe shelter. We may take time to observe that this widowed mother is almost deified by the moral teachers of the Japanese nation for having sacrificed her honor to secure the release of her own aged mother from prison. That is to say, she achieved her filial "duty" by the surrender of her virtue at the behest of the Taira tyrant, wherefore she is still belauded as an exalted moral example. The hostile chieftain spared the lives of her children, but endeavored to cloister them in convents, so that they would be out of his way. But Yoshitsune, like Emerson, would not be a priest. The pious Buddhist friars to whose care he had been committed were scandalized by his boisterous pranks, and called him, in horror, "the young ox." They were vastly relieved when at length he ran away with an ironmonger, whose life he straightway saved by exploits of the most heroic order. Destiny ordained that he should be reared to manhood in the family of a Fujiwara nobleman, under whose tutorship he developed unusual military ability, together with a high sense of chivalry. Meanwhile, the elder brother had become the leader of the Minamoto hosts, and the youthful Bayard laid his splendid services freely at his feet. It was due to his prowess that the decisive battle was won, in the straits of Shimonoseki, in the year A.D. 1185. But the elder brother became jealous of Yoshitsune's fame, as Saul was jealous of the loyal David; and, in spite of an appeal filled with the most touching and chivalrous eloquence, he was outlawed, a price was set upon his head, and he disappeared as a ruined fugitive whose end is shrouded in mystery. The Ainu in Yezo revere his name to this day as that of a demigod, so that many think that he spent his last days among them. His brother had power to end his career, but not to impair his future fame. He remains one of the chief of the Japanese national heroes, the final touch of romance being added to his story by the cruel injustice that caused his light to go out in darkness.

The decisive battle that Yoshitsune won for his brother in the Shimonoseki Straits (1185) is the greatest naval vic- The Minamoto tory in the annals of Japanese Victory. warfare. Yoshitsune had so pressed the Taira foe that he literally forced them to take water. Having besieged and burned the two great castles that constituted their final foothold, he drove the entire clan—men, women, and children, with the infant Emperor in their midst—to flee for safety to their fleet of five hundred vessels. Then, hastily collecting seven hundred vessels of his own, he crowded them with fighting-men and hurried on to the fray. Every soul on either side knew that the fight was to the death. The desperate Taira struck the first blow. Yoshitsune dominated and empowered his men like the spirit of war incarnate. There befell a fierce frenzy of slaughter. When the two sides had fought to exhaustion, there came a pause like a gasp for breath. But suddenly a great archer from among the Minamoto hosts sprang to his feet and sped a mighty shaft with such fierce ardor from his mighty bow that it clove the wooden prow of a Taira vessel as though it were human flesh. Instantly the men on either side leaped to their arms again, but stood for a moment motionless to watch the dramatic duel into which the great struggle had now suddenly resolved itself. For the chieftain in the Taira vessel plucked the shaft from the cloven prow

AN ANCIENT JAPANESE ARCHER.

and flung it to his doughtiest archer with the shout,—

"Shoot it back!"

The command was obeyed with such furious precision that a Minamoto soldier fell transfixed. Now it was Yoshitsune himself who gave the swift command,—

"Shoot it back!"

"It is but short and frail," calmly replied the Minamoto archer who had opened this strange duel, as he plucked the weapon from the dead man's breast and tossed it into the sea. Then, seizing a still longer shaft, he shot it with such fierce fury that it leaped through the armor and heart of a Taira bowman and fell far in the sea beyond. This was the signal for a general attack from the Minamoto legions beside which the earlier fighting was a mockery. Yoshitsune himself towered like Mars above his devoted bowmen, speeding each great shaft from his bowstring straight to the heart of his victim. "The whizzing of arrows, the clash of two-handed swords, the clanging of armor, the sweep of churning oars, the crash of colliding junks, the wild song of the rowers, the shouts of the warriors, made the storm-chorus of battle. One after another the Taira ships,

crushed by the prows of their opponents, or
scuttled by the iron bolt-heads of the Minamoto archers, sunk beneath the bubbling
waters, leaving red whirlpools of blood."
The battle over, those few who escaped the
red maw of the sea were pursued and ruth-
lessly slain. Only a handful reached the
mountain fastnesses of Kyūshū, where their
descendants still survive as a separate and
lonely community, suspicious of all their
kind, because their transmitted memories
have been so fiercely seared with the hot
breath of that terrible battle.

Treachery had a hand in the events of that
awful day. A traitor to the Tairas singled
out for Yoshitsune the precious central vessel that contained the sacred person of the
infant Emperor, with his mother and aged
grandmother. "Perhaps the annals of no
other country are richer in the recitals of
results gained by treachery," says Dr. Griffis
in "The Mikado's Empire." But when the
Minamoto clan bore down upon the imperial
boat and boarded it, Yoshitsune leading the
way, the grandmother of the Emperor, herself a Taira, leaped with him into the sea
rather than give his coveted person to the
foe, and his mother also was slain; but Yori-

tomo had already found a way to fill his place by having the infant Emperor's brother proclaimed Emperor in his stead.

Yoritomo was the unbrotherly chieftain whom Yoshitsune so faithfully served. Finding himself now master of the empire, he turned to the tasks of rule. The

Yoritomo.

result of his successful efforts at statecraft was to establish that peculiar form of government known as the Shōgunate, which ruled Japan almost continuously until the pristine imperialism was again restored as the outcome of Perry's expedition,—that is to say, during the seven hundred years embraced between the dates 1185 and 1868 A.D. The name *Shōgun* had long been in use; it simply meant "general." But General Yoritomo gave to this word a new meaning and became the first of the real Shōguns, or military rulers of feudal Japan. The first peculiarities of this dual system of government have already been made plain. Since the advent of Chinese bureaucratic influences, five hundred years before, the Emperor had been but a puppet in the hands of the dominant family, and for a century now this domination had been determined by martial power. Yoritomo developed this domination into a highly organized system known as the Shōgunate, and it became the permanent rule.

The gist of the Shōgunate system lies in the idea of two capitals. Since the year A.D.

The Shōgunate. 794 the Emperor and court had resided in Kyōto,—now sometimes called Saikyō, "the western capital,"— a splendid city in western Japan. But Yoritomo built for himself (A.D. 1189) a great city on the eastern coast, named Kamakura, which became the virtual capital of all Japan. Yet he knew the bee-like sentiment of the Japanese towards their emperor, hence he was ever careful to see that Kamakura received the sanction of Kyōto, to which it remained theoretically subordinate. But only theoretically so. Did not the reigning Emperor owe his very throne to Yoritomo? And not only that, but the empire was indebted to the Minamoto family for the addition to the realm of large portions of eastern and northern Japan which they had conquered from the ever retreating Ainu. We are confronted, therefore, by a condition and a theory, and an attempt to harmonize the two. The theory was, and always has been, that the Emperor, as "Son of Heaven," is supreme head of the realm. The condition was, that Yoritomo in fact was at the head of the realm. And the solution was the Shōgunate. Yoritomo, whose loyalty was certainly equalled by his astuteness, centred his power in his Eastern capital, Kamakura, but derived his authority from the Western capital of Kyōto. First, he secured consent from his Emperor to control the revenues. Then he established, with imperial assent, a judiciary. Next he achieved the appointment of his own relatives as military governors of provinces. Then, by the levying of special taxes,—always with the imperial consent,—he provided for a standing army; and so his system was complete. The sentimental capital was in Kyōto, where the Emperor dwelt in mysterious seclusion, and the practical capital was at Kamakura, where the Shōgun actively governed. That was the beginning of the Shōgunate and its essential idea. To make the fact still clearer, we may anticipate by pointing out that when the Shōgunate finally ceased to be, so did one of the capitals. Tōkyō (then called Yedo) became the Shōgun's capital in 1603, while the Emperor continued to reside at Kyōto. But when the Shōgunate fell two and a half centuries later, the Emperor himself came to Tōkyō, "the

Eastern Capital," which has since been the single centre of a fully restored imperialism.

After Yoritomo's death, the Shōgunate experienced a temporary eclipse. It was one of The Hōjō the revenges of fate. The same Usurpation. treatment which the Minamoto family had given to the Emperor was now administered to themselves. Just as the Emperor was in their hands, so they, decadent, fell into the hands of the powerful Hōjō family, connections of theirs by marriage. For a hundred and thirty-four years (A.D. 1199–1333) this high-handed Hōjō regency controlled the degenerate Shōgunate, which was supposed to be subordinate to the Emperor, who, however, was generally a feeble infant surrounded by a corrupt and venal court. The Hōjō rulers treated imperialism with scant respect, using force if there was need for it, and even sending one emperor, who dared to assert his rights, into an ignominious exile. It was the darkest period of the national history, and the name of Hōjō is forever execrable to loyal Japanese, because this hated household dared to commit the unpardonable crime of using force against the sacred person where others had used only "diplomacy."

The Hōjō interregnum is memorable for one great event, however, wherein the nation takes pride. It was the repulse of the great Tatar invasion in A.D. 1281. The Tatar Invasion. Kublai Khan, having conquered the throne of China, determined to conquer also Japan. With colossal self-assurance, he therefore despatched an embassy to Kamakura, demanding the peaceful subjection of the country. But his emissaries were treated by the Hōjō rulers with the most indignant scorn. Surprised that so small a nation should despise his sway, but tolerant of their pitiful ignorance, the tyrannous ruler of China now concluded to admonish them by means of an object lesson. So his troops took possession of Tsushima, a Japanese island midway between Japan and Korea. A second embassy was then despatched to Kamakura, with the intimation that as the troops had occupied Tsushima, so also would they overrun Japan. But the answer of the Hōjō regents was more emphatic than before,—they cut off the ambassadors' heads. Kublai Khan, now thoroughly enraged, thereupon prepared an armada of a hundred thousand men, which was destined, however, to share the fate of that other famous armada despatched later by

Spain against England. For when the invading fleet appeared in the offing of Hakata, on the coast of central Kyūshū, the valorous defence of the Japanese was aided and perfected by a terrible storm, or typhoon, which overwhelmed the invaders with destruction. This is the only time that an actual invasion of Japan has been attempted, and the sole lustre of the Hōjō rule is that reflected on it from this great naval victory.

The ruler whom the Hōjōs had exiled—greatest of all Japanese emperors—eventually had his revenge. Aided by large loyal forces under two indignant generals, this vigorous exiled monarch, Go-Daigo, accomplished the overthrow of the Hōjō power, with the complete destruction of Kamakura, in the year 1333. To-day, as one walks through the bamboo thickets, or bathes in the peaceful surf of this little fishing village, it is almost impossible to realize that here was once a city of a million souls. However, Yoritomo's great lonesome Buddha remains in token of the vanished grandeur, contemplating with his downcast golden eyes the stately passage of the centuries.

A Brief Imperialism.

Yoritomo's magnificent monument at

Kamakura is also the most notable monument of Japanese art. It is the immense bronze image of Amida (Sanscrit, Metal Art in Japan. Amitâbha), the deity of boundless light, but commonly known as the *Dai Butsu*, or Great Buddha. It is worthy of our especial attention because it represents the highest Japanese attainment in the art wherein they have especially excelled, that is, the art of metal work.

That bronze was imported from China into Japan is proved by its very name, *Kara-gane*, or "China metal." And that this importation was made at a very early day is evinced by the fact that bronzes reached a high development in Japan fully a thousand years ago. The colossal effigy of Buddha The Great Buddhas. that still exists at Nara, most ancient of the permanent capitals, was completed in the year 749 A.D. It is larger than the one at Kamakura, being fifty-three feet in height, and the very largest idol in the world; but it is far inferior in point of artistic merit.

Bronze work, therefore, reached its utmost acme in Japan during the Kamakura period; for in this old-time capital one finds not only Yoritomo's wondrous monument, but another great achievement in metal that rivals it in consummate skill and splendor. As for the Buddha itself the prior in charge informs us that it was cast in September, 1252, by the celebrated glyptic artist Ōno Gorōyemon, under the general direction of one of the ladies who had been attached to Yoritomo's court, and in fulfilment of what she knew to be his cherished desire. It is almost fifty feet in height and is ninety-eight feet in circumference; the width of the eyes, which are of pure gold, is four feet each; the length of the ear is six and a half feet; and the great silver boss upon the forehead weighs thirty pounds avoirdupois. Construction was accomplished by means of sheets of bronze cast separately, brazed together, and finished off at the edges with a chisel. But no figures and no description can do justice to the supreme impressiveness of this gigantic work of art, which seems to grow in grandeur, like Niagara, with every visit.* The ideality of Ōno's conception has not been marred by the colossal scale on which he wrought. Somehow the image conveys far better than words the essential mes-

---

* An illustration of the *Dai Butsu* is contained in the companion volume, "Japan To-Day."

sage of the higher Buddhism. As one gazes, awe-struck, and with upturned face, into the profoundly calm and benignant countenance, whose features speak so eloquently of absolute self-conquest and self-repression, this "fleeting show" of mundane existence seems as but a show of trifling shadows in comparison with the Nirvana of the vast Unknown. Perhaps no other image in the world to-day testifies with mightier power to the message that inspired the hand of the author.

The other most eloquent witness of Japan's great bronze age, so to speak, is found within this same small fishing village; reminding one of the poet's proverb, "Oft within a wooden house a golden room we find." Mr. Lafcadio Hearn's description of this golden Kwannon goddess is so vivid and so beautiful that it is quoted here, in part, from his "Glimpses of Unfamiliar Japan."—"The old priest lights a lantern, and leads the way through a low doorway into the interior of the temple, into some very lofty darkness. I follow him cautiously a while, discerning nothing whatever but the flicker of the lantern; then we halt before something which gleams. A moment, and my

The Golden Goddess of Mercy.

eyes, becoming more accustomed to the darkness, begin to distinguish outlines; the
gleaming object defines itself as a foot, and I
perceive the hem of a golden robe undulating
over the instep. Now the other foot appears;
the figure is certainly standing. I can perceive that we are in a narrow but also very
lofty chamber, and that out of some mysterious blackness overhead ropes are dangling
down into the circle of lantern light illumi-
nating the golden feet. The priest lights two
more lanterns, and suspends them upon
hooks attached to a pair of pendent ropes
about a yard apart; then he pulls up both together slowly. More of the golden robe is
revealed as the lanterns ascend, swinging on
their way; then the outlines of two mighty
knees; then the curving of columnar thighs
under chiselled drapery, and as with the still
waving ascent of the lanterns the golden
vision towers higher through the gloom, ex-
pectation intensifies. There is no sound but
the sound of invisible pulleys overhead,
which squeak like bats. Now above the
golden girdle, the suggestion of a bosom.
Then the glowing of a golden hand uplifted
in benediction. Then another golden hand
holding a lotus. And at last a face, golden,

smiling with eternal youth and infinite tenderness,—the face of Kwannon.

"So revealed out of the consecrated darkness, this ideal of Divine femininity, creation of a forgotten art and time, is more than impressive. I can scarcely call the emotion which it produces admiration; it is rather reverence.

"But the lanterns, which paused a while at the level of the beautiful face, now ascend still higher, with a fresh squeaking of pulleys. And lo! the tiara of the divinity appears, with strangest symbolism. It is a pyramid of heads, of faces,—charming faces of maidens, miniature faces of Kwannon herself.

"For this is the Kwannon of the Eleven Faces,—Jiū-ichi-men-Kwannon."

So by the side of the deity of boundless light, the Mother of Mercy stands hid in the inky darkness, waiting with her bright golden smile for such as will lift up the torches of prayer. Nowhere else in Japan do the pagan religions wear such beneficent aspect, or promise so much of sweet mercy. Nowhere else in the world, let us say, has sculptured art lent more aid to devoutness.

Japan owes her art wholly to Buddhism, as

we shall see still more clearly when we come to consider her painting. But it is none the less true of her statuary; for the great religion of India has peopled the Japanese solitudes with statues, and chiselled even the wayside rocks with texts from the sûtras. One traveller speaks for the many when he asks with enthusiasm, "Who can forget the soft enchantment of this Buddhist atmosphere?—the deep music of the great bells?—the green peace of gardens haunted by fearless things: doves that flutter down at call, fishes rising to be fed?" Buddhism is a religion not so much of ethics as of esthetics; and this largely accounts for its successes among a people with whom beauty is divine. Their modern metalwork, in minor departments, has become familiar in the West. They are especially notable for a remarkable amalgam known as *shakudō*, which appears to consist chiefly of iron, relieved by partial overlayings of gold, silver, and bronze. The designs into which these amalgams are wrought still bear the tracery of Buddhism. Not the least of the Japanese metallic achievements have been suits of remarkable armor, sometimes thinly overlaid with gold here and there; and we

Artistic Influence of Buddhism.

A TEMPLE GARDEN IN KYŌTO.

gain a vivid realization of Japan's modern progress when we reflect that this cunningly wrought but cumbersome armor has been worn into warfare by men still alive. Perhaps the most crafty of the bygone artists was Miyochin Munechika, " who loved to set himself impossible tasks, and who manipulated iron as though it were wax." Modern He has worthy modern successors in Masters. Saito and Suzuki, men devoted to the highest ideals of their craft.

But let us resume the thread of our narrative.

The downfall of the Hōjō power (1333) meant the complete collapse of the Shōgunate, and the Emperor now found him- The Ashikaga self restored to absolute power. Clan. But the restoration of imperialism was of very brief duration. Go-Daigo bestowed great power upon a man named Ashikaga, kinsman of the Minamoto clan, and this prince of intrigue and treachery contrived to erect a new Shōgunate, with himself as chief. His main step to this end was to oppose the Emperor who had exalted him to power, even to the extent of setting up a rival emperor whom he himself could control. This plunged the nation once more into the horrors of a bloody civil war, which lasted about sixty years. It was the war of the rival Mikados, and has been called the Japanese War of the Roses. The strife ended in the year 1392, with the triumph of the Ashikaga party, so that the Shōgunate was now fully restored to power, and the emperors again became puppets. The rule of the Ashikaga family continued until 1565, when they met the fate of their predecessors, the Fujiwara, succumbing to their own effeminacy. But meanwhile their reign was noted for the advancement of artistic elegance, just as the Fujiwara *régime* had fostered literature. Painting and the drama flourished, while those peculiar Japanese arts that have to do with flowers were at this time brought to perfection. The elaborate tea ceremonials, known as *cha-yu,** also had their ori-

---

* "The tea used is in the form, not of tea-leaves, but of powder, so that the resulting beverage resembles pea-soup in color and consistency. There is a thicker kind called *koi-cha,* and a thinner kind called *usu-cha.* The former is used in the earlier stage of the proceedings, the latter towards the end. The tea is made and drunk in a preternaturally slow and formal manner, each action, each gesture, being fixed by an elaborate code of rules. Every article connected with the ceremony, such as the tea-canister, the incense-burner, the hanging scroll, and the bouquet of flowers in the alcove, is either handled, or

ARMOR USED IN "THE WAR OF THE ROSES."

gin at the court of the Ashikaga, which seemed to delight in the furtherance of strange and esoteric arts. Buddhism, moreover, reached its height of power at this period. But throughout the remoter provinces a condition approaching anarchy prevailed for the most of the time, while piracy flourished on the seas.

The Ashikaga regency, if notable for artistic excellence, was also notorious for governmental misrule.

The art of painting reached its highest development under the Ashikaga rule, having been introduced and fostered by the Buddhists. The native religion, Shintō, had no art. Its ghost-houses, silent and void, were not even decorated, and they retain their pristine simplicity to this

The Art of Painting: Its Origin.

---

else admired at a distance, in ways and with phrases which unalterable usage prescribes. Even the hands are washed, the room is swept, a little bell is rung, and the guests walk from the house to the garden and from the garden back into the house, at stated times and in a stated manner which never varies, except in so far as certain schools, as rigidly conservative as monkish confraternities, obey slightly varying rules of their own, handed down from their ancestors."—CHAMBERLAIN. " Things Japanese."

day. But Buddhism, as Mr. Hearn observes, —himself a Buddhist,—brought in its train from China all of the arts of carving, painting, and decoration, giving especial attention to painting. "The images of its Bodhisattvas, smiling in gold,—the figures of its heavenly guardians and infernal judges, its feminine angels and monstrous demons,—must have startled and amazed imaginations yet unaccustomed to any kind of art. Great paintings hung in the temples, and frescoes limned upon their walls or ceilings, explained better than words the doctrine of the Six States of Existence, and the dogma of future rewards and punishments. In rows of *kakemono*, suspended side by side, were displayed the incidents of a Soul's journey to the realm of judgment, and all the horrors of the various hells. One pictured the ghosts of faithless wives, for ages doomed to pluck, with bleeding fingers, the rasping bamboo-grass that grows by the Springs of Death; another showed the torment of the slanderer, whose tongue was torn by demon-pincers; in a third appeared the spectres of lustful men, vainly seeking to flee the embraces of women of fire, or climbing, in frenzied terror, the slopes of the Mountain of Swords. Pictured also were the circles of the Preta-world [*gaki*], and the pangs of the Hungry Ghosts, and likewise the pains of rebirth in the form of reptiles and of beasts. And the art of these early representations—many of which have been preserved—was an art of no mean order. We can hardly conceive the effect upon inexperienced imagination of the crimson frown of Emma, judge of the dead,—or the vision of that weird Mirror which reflected to every spirit the misdeeds of its life in the body,—or the monstrous fancy of that double-faced Head before the judgment seat, representing the visage of the woman Mirume, whose eyes behold all secret sin; and the vision of the man Kaguhana, who smells all odors of evil-doing. Parental affection must have been deeply touched by the painted legend of the world of children's ghosts,— the little ghosts that must toil, under demon surveillance, in the Dry Bed of the River of Souls. But pictured terrors were offset by pictured consolations,—by the beautiful figure of Kwannon, white Goddess of Mercy,— by the compassionate smile of Jizō, the playmate of infant ghosts,—by the charm also of celestial nymphs, floating on iridescent wings in light of azure. The Buddhist painters opened to simple fancy the palaces of heaven, and guided hope, through gardens of jewel-trees, even to the shores of that lake where the souls of the blessed are reborn in lotos-blossoms, and tended by angel-nurses.'' So truly exotic is the art of painting that Japanese art-critics still give only grudging recognition to the leading native artists in comparison with the praise bestowed so lavishly on Chinese masters.

The earliest native painter to attain renown was Kose no Kanaoka, who flourished Artistic during the latter half of the ninth Limitations. century, under the patronage of the Fujiwara courtiers. If we could believe half of the quaint legends that testify to the effect of his skill on his contemporaries, we should have to accord him a place among the few great artists of the world. But pre-eminent rank cannot be accorded even to the greatest of Japanese painters,—as Sesshū and Hokusai, for example,—except in the minor branches of their art, such as decoration, in which they excel. Mr. Alfred East, when lecturing on the native art in Tōkyō, tersely expressed the facts in declaring it to be ''great in small things, but small in great things.'' And Professor Chamberlain ampli-

AN ARTIST AT WORK.

fies this criticism when he says, ''The Japanese are undoubtedly Raphaels of fishes, and
insects, and flowers, and bamboo-stems
swaying in the breeze; and they have given
us charming fragments of idealized scenery.
But they have never succeeded in adequately
transferring to canvas 'the human form divine;' they have never made grand historical
scenes live again before the eyes of posterity;
they have never, like the early Italian masters, drawn away men's hearts from earth to
heaven in an ecstasy of adoration.''

By an interesting coincidence, Japanese
painting attained its acme synchronously
with Italian art—that is to say, The Classic
during the fifteenth century. It was School.
then that Sesshū flourished (1421–1507), the
greatest Japanese master of the Chinese
school. Anderson, in his great work on ''The
Pictorial Arts of Japan,'' says that ''it is
difficult for a European to appreciate Sesshū
at his true value. . . . Notwithstanding the
boast of the artist that the scenery of China
was his only teacher and the credit bestowed
upon him by his admirers of having invented
a new style, he has in no respect departed
from the artificial rules accepted by his fel-
low painters. He was, however, an original

and powerful artist, and his renderings of Chinese scenes bear evidences of local study that we look for in vain in the works of his successors. The grand simplicity of·his landscape compositions, their extraordinary breadth of design, the illusive suggestions of atmosphere and distance, and the all-pervading sense of poetry, demonstrate a genius that could rise above all defects of theory in the principles of his art." Sesshū and his artistic contemporaries—Chō Deusu, "the Fra Angelico of Japan;" Jōsetsu, famous for his flowers and birds; with Shūbun, and the Kano succession—these constitute the brightest galaxy of the classical school of painters, and give great brilliancy to the treacherous Ashikaga rule.

The *Yamato Ryū*, or "Japanese school" of painting, had been established about·the
The Native year 1000 by an independent artist
School. named Motomitsu. Two centuries later it became known as the Tosa School, and came largely under the influences of classicism. But it had planted the seeds of a distinctively native art, being characterized by those Japanesque peculiarities to which Westerners have now become accustomed, with its "neglect of perspective, its impossible

mountains, its quaint dissection of roofless interiors.'' Toba Sōjō, in the middle of the twelfth century, wrought its coarse humor to a high degree of artistic effectiveness, the *Toba-e*, or ''Toba pictures,'' constituting a school of their own. The classicist Mitsunobu, however, is accounted the leader of the Tosa painters. But, towards the end of the sixteenth century, an artist of the Tosa school, Iwasa Matahei by name, emphasized the earlier traditions of the *Yamato Ryū;* and a hundred years later great impetus was given to the development of a purely native art by the realist Hishigawa Moronobu, with his book illustrations in color. This line of development continued through Ōkyo, in the eighteenth century, and Sosen, his pupil, until at last, under the Tokugawa régime (if we may anticipate), ''art was released from its mediæval Chinese swaddling-clothes, and allowed to mix in the society of living men and women.'' Then it was that a great multitude of ''artisan-artists'' sprang up, who brought about the popularization of Japanese art by the naturalness of their method, and by their conformity to the taste of the public.

Foreign students of Japanese painting are likely to be most strongly attracted by the work of the artist Hokusai (1760–1849), the chief of these artisan-artists, and most nota-

Hokusai. ble of all native painters. Living in extremest poverty, and creating art for art's sake, his extraordinary talent covered "the whole range of Japanese art motives," as Dr. Anderson tells us,—"scenes of history, drama, and novel, incidents in the daily life of his own class, realizations of familiar objects of animal and vegetable life, wonderful suggestions of the scenery of his beloved Yedo and its surroundings, and a hundred other inspirations that would require a volume to describe." One of his best known works is a collection called *Fuji Hyakkei*, or "A Hundred Views of Mt. Fuji," executed when he was seventy-six years old. He depicts the peerless mountain from every possible—and impossible—point of view, one of the sketches even showing how the mountain looks while being ascended by a fiery dragon. Thousands of Hokusai's sketches are still extant, all of them possessing a certain boldness of conception and vigor of line that mark them with the touch of the master. His chief contemporaries in color-print work were Toyokuni, Kunisada, Shigenobu, and Hiroshige. It is significant that he died just four years previous to the coming of Commodore Perry, and that his death marked the decay of pictorial art in Japan. Since the opening of her hermit gates to the workaday business of the modern world, Japan has had little time to paint pictures. There are still men who work before easels, but that leisurely composure is gone without which painting ceases to exist as an art, and sinks to the level of mechanics. Decorators there are, in abundance, who turn out *pretty* works by the score; but the glory of Japanese painting, which reached its classic zenith in the fifteenth century, and its highest native development under Hokusai, is dimmed by material matters.

The distinctive influence of this art, however, can never be lost from the world. It is marked, above all, by natural- Features of ness. This is true even of those Japanese Art. features that seem to us almost unnatural. The invention of the instantaneous photograph, for example, proved that the "awkward" Japanese artist was not awkward at all, but that he had really caught, in some inexplicable manner, the true report of figures in rapid motion, as seems in no wise possible for the slower Occidental eye. Then he takes this photographic report and idealizes it, with a result that is unique in art. It may not be great, but it is wonderful and very beautiful. The chief reason of this wonder and beauty is found in the fact—to quote from Sir Rutherford Alcock—"that the Japanese have derived all their fundamental ideas of symmetry, so different from ours, from a close study of nature and of her processes in the attainment of endless variety."

They are teaching us the beauty of the irregular in art, which they have learned from the irregularity of nature. The arrangement of a Japanese bouquet, for example, is as different from the method of one of our florists as nature differs from artifice. Instead of forcing the poor flowers into stilted straight-jacket rigidity, the Japanese florist jealously maintains their sweet freedom, conserving in the cut bouquet the charm and the grace of free nature. So also, while their painted birds and flowers are doubtless not afflicted with ornithological or botanical correctness, they invariably evince a profound devotion to the irregular beauty of nature that cannot be too much admired. Because the Japanese artist is loyal to nature, he avoids geometrical artifice. "Thus if a lacquer box in the form

d idealizes it, with
... It may not be
and very beauti-
... wonder and
... quote from Sir
... Japanese have
... ideas of sym-
..., from a close
r processes in the
...

... beauty of the
... learned from
... The arrangement
example, is as dif-
... of our florists
... Instead of
... stilted straight-
a florist jealously
... conserving in
... and the grace of
... their painted
... not afflicted
... correctness,
... devotion to
... that cannot be
... the Japanese art-
... geometrical
... box in the form

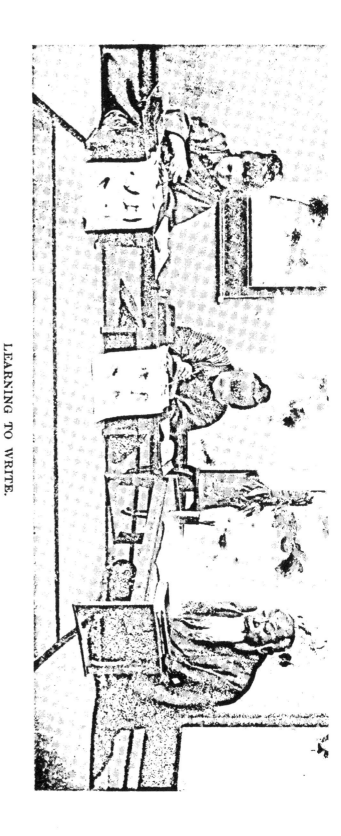

LEARNING TO WRITE.

of a parallelogram is the object, the artists will not divide it in two equal parts by a perpendicular line, but by a diagonal, as offering a more pleasing line and division. If the box be round they will seek to lead the eye away from the naked regularity of the circle by a pattern distracting attention, as, for example, by a zigzag breaking the circular outline, and supported by other ornaments.''

The characteristic freedom and grace of execution may doubtless be traced very largely to the commonplace fact that a brush and not a pen is the immemorial instrument of writing. From childhood the artist handles the brush, so that he is not compelled to acquire, in the less flexible years of maturity, skill in the use of a new instrument. He can hardly remember the time when his hand and the brush were not cronies. Not only so, but from the beginning he has been tracing the most intricate free-hand figures, in the complex ideographs of his cumbersome alphabet. Their caligraphic system of penmanship makes all Japanese more or less artists. Behind this, of course, lies that delicate esthetic temperament which is one of the marked characteristics of the race, as also their faculties of close observation.

When all is said, possibly the most pleasing and most truly artistic feature of the better Japanese painting is the fact that it does not assert, but suggests. It credits the critic with imagination, and permits him to use it, thus sharing the artist's own joy of creation. It is not photography, it is poetry; it is not mechanics, but art.

The Ashikaga reign is chiefly memorable in history for the beginning of European con- tact with Japan, through the ship-wreck of three Portuguese sailors on the southernmost island of Kyūshū in the year 1542. A few years later Mendez Pinto twice visited this empire, which Marco Polo had so extravagantly described to his countrymen upon the basis of Chinese hearsay, about two centuries before. Pinto and his companions remained in Japan for months together, introducing the use of firearms, which the people were quick to imitate, and astounding the natives with the efficacy of European surgery and drugs. A number of words that have now become ingrained in the Japanese vocabulary can be traced back to this early influx of European commodities which brought their own strange nomenclature with them.

When Pinto was on the point of leaving Japan in the year 1547, a Japanese by the name of Anjirō, with his servant, The First Missionary. succeeded in embarking with him. This runaway adventure resulted in nothing less than the successful introduction of Christianity. For Anjirō and his companion were carried by Pinto to Malacca, where the great Jesuit missionary, Francis Xavier, happened to meet them. He became deeply interested in the two Japanese, and soon won them to the Christian faith. Having given them a course of instruction in the seminary at Goa, he himself returned with them in 1549, landing at Kagōshima in Kyūshū on the fifteenth day of August. Xavier brought with him two zealous Portuguese assistants, and the first converts to be won were those of Anjirō's own household. The prince of the province of Satsuma, whereof Kagōshima is the capital, gave great assistance to the missionaries, who were most favorably impressed with their reception. "I really think," wrote Xavier in early letters, "that among barbarous nations there can be none that has more natural goodness than Japan. ... They are wonderfully inclined to see all that is good and honest, and have an eagerness to learn. . . . This nation is the delight of my soul.'' This zealous, self-denying, and sympathetic missionary met with great success in the prosecution of his mission. He went everywhere preaching the Word. Crossing over from Kyūshū into the main island of Hondo, he journeyed from town to town, and even reached the imperial capital, Kyōto, where he failed to gain a hearing at the court, but, nothing daunted, proclaimed the gospel to the crowds in the street. Remaining in Japan for two years and three months, he then embarked on a mission to China, but died on the way, at the age of forty-six years. His work in Japan survived him, and grew to enormous proportions. We are told that by the year 1582 there were a hundred and thirty-eight Jesuit missionaries, with six hundred thousand converts. By the time the century closed, this number is said to have increased to a million,—the flourishing city of Nagasaki, for example, containing hardly a single citizen who was not a Christian. But troublous times awaited the Christians in the incoming century, when the commingling of politics with religion, of Church and State, brought about an explosion that resulted practically in the destruction of the Roman Catholic Church in Japan.

The close of the sixteenth century witnessed the extinction of the nerveless Ashikaga Shōgunate, and the emergence of that great Japanese triumvirate whose successive careers marked an interregnum of individualism, and became in turn the foundation of a Shōgunate which both brought this peculiar system to its splendid climax, and also at length yielded to a complete and final overthrow. These three great men were Nobunaga, known as the persecutor of the Buddhists; Hideyoshi, or Taikō-Sama, sometimes called the Japanese Napoleon; and Iyeyasu, the great founder of the Tokugawa Shōgunate and the builder of Tōkyō. Both Hideyoshi and Iyeyasu stained their reigns with bloody persecutions of the Christians.

The Great Triumvirate.

Nobunaga, a descendant of the defeated Taira clan, came of a family of Shintō priests. But he, like Yoshitsune before him, forsook the altar for the camp. The misrule of the Ashikaga Shōgunate had allowed Japan to sink into a desperate condition of feudal anarchy, when might made right, and tenure of land was decided by force

Nobunaga.

of arms alone. His baronial father bestowed on Nobunaga wide acres that had been bought and held through battle. The doughty son (A.D. 1533–1582) speedily doubled and redoubled his possessions until he controlled a greater power than the Shōgun. This title, however, he never usurped, being loyal to the defeat of his ancestors. But he set his own Shōgun on the throne; and afterwards, having quarrelled with him, deposed him and his family altogether (A.D. 1573), after the Ashikaga had ruled for two hundred and thirty-eight years. There is something sublime in the pride of this Taira chieftain, who, scorning the support of the system that had been set up by his clan's most ancient foe, ruled by sheer individual strength alone. But he was warrior rather than statesman. He lacked the diplomacy necessary to make good his conquests, and at length paid dearly for his soldierly roughness. Being one day in an especially rollicking humor, he tucked an officer's head under his arm and beat on it with a fan for a drumstick. The sensitive captain never forgot the insult, and when the time came he had his revenge.

But Nobunaga lived forty-nine years, and made an imperishable fame before his sensitive captain betrayed him. His chief distinction is somewhat invidious; his is the best hated name in the Buddhist "index expurgatorius." It was in- Persecutions of the Buddhists, evitable that he and the Buddhists should disagree, for in his march towards organized power he found them the most powerful organization in feudal mediæval Japan. They had built great temples that were really castles, and the cowl was often the covering of a coat-of-mail. One of the most powerful emperors is reputed to have said that there were three objects he could not control,—the throw of the dice in play, the waters of a certain rough river, and the monks in the great monastery of Mount Hiei. There were myriads of them. The sacred precincts, always secure from invasion on account of the reverence felt for religion, enclosed no less than three thousand buildings. Unfriendly to Nobunaga on account of his haughty independence, the abbot gave shelter and aid to his enemies. Nobunaga seized the opportunity to make open war upon the great organization of Buddhism,—the individual against the institution. His generals were at first dumfounded that he should declare battle upon the holy religion of Buddha, but he won them to his will, and in 1571 burned the vast monastery, slaughtering or banishing the monks. Subsequently he besieged and destroyed the great monastic castle of Hongwanji, in Ōsaka, with a ruthless slaughter of its twenty thousand inmates. These two immense properties belong to the government to this day, while Buddhism has never been able quite to recover its ancient strength.

Enmity against Buddhism made Nobunaga friendly to the Christians. The Roman Catholic missionaries of the period described him as "a prince of large stature, but of a weak and delicate complexion, with a heart and soul that supplied all other wants; ambitious above all mankind; brave, generous, and bold, and not without many excellent moral virtues; inclined to justice, and an enemy to treason." Although never a convert to the Christian faith, he remained its friend and patron throughout life, and in the very year of his death (1582) caused a splendid embassy to be sent to Portugal, Spain, and Rome, where they were received with great magnificence and decorated as "knights of the gilded spears." Christianity reached the acme of its temporal

Patronage of Christianity.

A WARRIOR MONK OF OLD JAPAN.

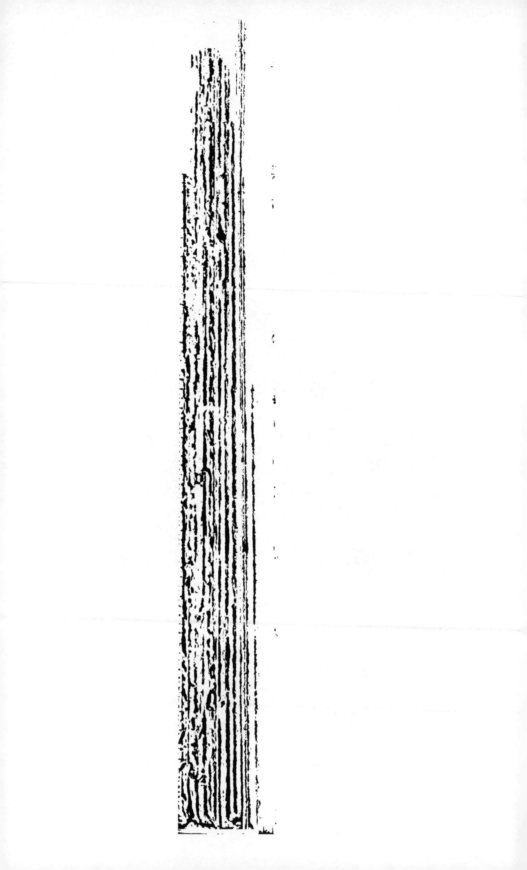

power in Japan under the patronage of this great enemy of the Buddhists.

While at the very height of his power, Nobunaga was betrayed by the man whose sensitive pride he had outraged. Having his headquarters in a confiscated Buddhist temple in Kyōto, while all of his loyal legions were away on the battle-field, he found himself surrounded one day by a troop of traitors, bought over for vengeance's sake by the promise of rich booty. Being struck by a hostile arrow from the hands of one of these men,—his own soldiers,—he realized the situation, and calmly proceeded to deprive his treacherous enemy of the sweetest morsel in the dish of revenge; for, having set the temple on fire, he plunged his own sword into his vitals, and his body was in ashes before it could be shamed by the touch of a treacherous hand.

Hideyoshi (A.D. 1536–1598) and Iyeyasu were Nobunaga's two leading generals. As soon as Hideyoshi heard of this foul deed, he hastened to Kyōto to avenge it. Riding in reckless advance of his troops in the ardor of his loyal anger, Hideyoshi himself escaped the same band of assassins only by means of a stratagem that

Hideyoshi

was characteristic of his entire career; for
the traitors were in ambuscade, and the gal-
loping horseman was suddenly surrounded.
He plunged blindly into a narrow lane that
led between two rice-fields, and, finding himself presently entrapped in the walled approach to a little temple, turned his horse
roundabout, stabbed him in the flank, and
sent him thundering madly back upon the
pursuers with such force that they were scattered pell-mell. Meanwhile, Hideyoshi hurried into the temple and found the monks
splashing together in their common daily bath.
Rapidly disrobing, he plunged in among them,
exhorting them at the same time to secrecy,
and when his pursuers presently arrived,
Hideyoshi was nowhere to be seen, but only
a great vat-full of naked, rollicking priests.
Later, when his own anxious troops reached
the temple, they found their leader compla-
cently awaiting their coming, sitting upon the
clean cool mats, refreshed by a bath from the
labor of his reckless ride. He afterwards
utterly routed the conspiracy of traitors,
whose leader died in the same manner as
the master whom he had betrayed.

Hideyoshi, who has the unique distinction
in Japanese history of being known as Taikō

Sama, "the Great Counsellor," is invested with additional human interest by the fact that in this mediæval empire of strict caste and ceremonial he presents an instance of a man rising to the utmost heights of power from an obscure and ignominious origin. Doubtless this feature of his career assists in making him to-day what he undoubtedly is,—the demigod of a new and a more democratic Japan, where the shining example of the Taikō serves as a beacon to many an ambitious youth. He was born of the commonest peasants, and in his boyhood became a monkey-faced groom. Thus by chance he came into Nobunaga's employ, who was attracted to him by his fascinating ugliness, as well as by his mischievous, bold pranks, and encouraged the clown to be a soldier. He rose rapidly to the rank of general, and with characteristic comedy made for himself a coat-of-arms. One can see in it a sane and mirthful mockery of the pretentious armorial bearings of the aristocratic generals who despised him. Hideyoshi found that his best friend on a hot and dusty march was his gourd-canteen, so he erected a calabash as his standard! When he would win a new battle, up would go another calabash, until an embroidered cluster of gourds finally became the inspiring banner of his ever victorious legions.

When Nobunaga was dead and avenged, Hideyoshi resolved to become his successor. This was far from an easy task in a land where heredity counted for everything. Nobunaga's two sons had powerful supporters, but Hideyoshi adopted a grandson of the dead prince, only an infant in arms, and succeeded in having him installed as successor, with Hideyoshi in the comfortable position of guardian. Upon this guardianship he based a claim to precedence over all princes and generals, which he established at the point of the sword.

In a series of brilliant campaigns this militant lord of the calabash brought all of Hondo under his sway, and then all of Kyūshū, including the lordly ruler of Satsuma. He possessed in marked degree those very qualities of statesmanship in which Nobunaga was markedly lacking. Instead of utterly humbling the vanquished and incurring their inveterate hatred, he allowed them to keep their lands, but in fief, as a favor from him as their "Counsellor." Thus he unified the entire realm for the first time in history, and laid the foundations for the great Tokugawa Shōgunate that was to be built up by his successor, Iyeyasu. Hideyoshi himself aspired to the office of Shōgun, but his low birth stood in his way. It is well for his fame that this is so, for his unique appellation of "Taikō" secures him a distinction that would have been obscured by a new line of Shōguns. He stands, like Napoleon, solitary in original power, distinguished for individual success in spite of the institutions that would have crushed him.

Hideyoshi was a man of no religion whatever. Like Nobunaga, he persecuted the Buddhists, and was inclined to be friendly to the Christians. But the Roman orders fell out among themselves, and this brought them into trouble with Hideyoshi. The Jesuits attempted to pre-empt Japan, and were aided by Papal authority. But this was distasteful to the Franciscans and Dominicans, who desired to reap their share of the harvest. Not only so, but commercial jealousies arose between Spaniards and Portuguese. Each party sought the partiality of Hideyoshi, whose suspicions were at length aroused against both. He became convinced that the

First Persecution of the Christians.

preaching of the gospel was but a pretext
for the conquest of the country. Accord-
ingly, in the year 1587 he issued an edict of
expulsion against all missionaries. This resulted, six years later, in the execution of
nine priests in Nagasaki, this being the first
persecution authorized under the government. Seventeen converts were slain with
the foreigners. But Hideyoshi does not seem
to have attempted the extermination of Christianity altogether. In fact, several of his
leading generals remained open confessors
of the faith. He appears only to have sought
the expulsion of all foreign influence, allowing the native church to take care of itself.

It was a Christian general who rendered
largest assistance to Hideyoshi in the most
The Invasion   ambitious undertaking of his life,
of Korea.   —the conquest of Korea. He was
a man of boundless aspirations. When first
he visited Kamakura and saw a wooden image of Yoritomo, he patted it familiarly on
the shoulder with the words, "You are my
friend. You achieved universal power, and
only I besides you have been able to do likewise (in Japan). But you came of a famous
family, while I am sprung from mere peasants. I intend at length to conquer all the

earth, including China. What do you think of that?" His invasion of Korea was intended to be only the beginning of a vast Napoleonic campaign.

A pretext was easily found. Under the enfeebled rule of the Ashikaga, the customary tribute had ceased to be collected from Korea, which Japan had long demanded on the basis of the traditional conquests of the Empress Jingō. In 1582 Hideyoshi sent an envoy to collect it, but without avail. Later on he sent another, who was so successful as to return with a Korean embassy to interview the Taikō. He treated this embassy with such contempt that his attitude towards their country could not be mistaken, and when the Koreans reached home they urged preparations for war. The "land of the morning calm," unhappily placed between the Scylla of China and the Charybdis of Japan, was as helpless then as it is to-day. Meanwhile, Hideyoshi collected from his vassal princes an army of three hundred thousand men, and prepared to despatch them to Korea. At that time, it may be remarked, the maritime power of his country was at its climax.

A characteristic obstacle prevented the

personal leadership of Hideyoshi: his aged mother sorrowing so that she could not eat, filial piety impelled him to remain at home. One of his two commanders was the Christian general, Konishi; the other being an unfriendly rival, named Katō. The Japanese armies were everywhere victorious, even when confronted by an army from China, which Korea had called to her assistance; but internal dissensions, originating with the two rival generals, were a source of great weakness with the Japanese. Finally, a truce was concluded, of course without Hideyoshi's knowledge or consent, China and Japan arranging the terms of the treaty, with no regard to the helpless little bone of contention. It seems that China granted to Hideyoshi the honor of investiture over Korea, while Japan on her part agreed to withdraw her troops and never to invade Korea again. But the peacemakers reckoned without their host. When the Taikō heard that his authority over abject Korea rested upon the consent of another country that he despised with equal hatred, he flew into a rage, and came near killing his own ambassador. He straightway opened the war afresh, and his sanguinary appetite was

THE EAR MOUND OF HIDEYOSHI.

somewhat satisfied upon the receipt of a
cargo of some forty thousand pickled ears
clipped from the heads of Korean and Chinese warriors. These relics of savage warfare were buried in a mound at Kyōto, which
may still be seen, surmounted by a stone monument called the Ear-Tomb.

This ruthless and fruitless warfare was
terminated by the death of the Taikō, which
occurred in 1598, his last words forming the
prayer: "Let not the spirits of the hundred
thousand troops I have sent to Korea become disembodied in a foreign land." His
ambitious undertakings appeal to the imagination alone. The true reason of his greatness rests upon his valuable achievements at
home. Besides the unification of the country,
he erected great public buildings, dug canals,
built bridges, and established that system
which developed into the daimiate of the
Iyeyasu Shōguns. What Napoleon was to
France, such was Hideyoshi to Japan.

The analogy holds good even in the matter
of art spoliation. Hideyoshi's Korean campaign ravaged that ancient kingdom so Ceramics.
thoroughly that it has never recovered. Porcelain, for example, has become a
lost art in Korea, because her great ancient

potters were transported bodily to Japan, and her own manufactures pre-empted. Japan had hitherto made but little real progress in ceramics; but no sooner had the Korean teachers arrived than the imitative genius of the people exerted itself to adapt and outdo the masters. Not only did the delicate art appeal especially to the peculiar artistic ability of this nation of esthetes, but they had material ready to their hands. "The islands, being mountainous, are rich in watercourses, which carry with them great quantities of sand, mixed with clay. Thus the nation has been furnished by nature with the numberless varieties of paste which are essential for good pottery."

Mr. Sadakichi Hartmann, from whose little work on "Japanese Art" this passage is quoted, reminds us that Arita, in Hideyoshi's native province of Hizen, was from the start, and is still to-day, the leading porcelain manufacturing town of Japan. The ware is called Imari, simply because Imari, at the head of the Gulf of Ōmura, is the principal shipping port for Arita's products. "The larger part of the pottery produced here is the underglazed blue and white combination which made Arita famous, and which was success-

THE DECORATION OF PORCELAIN.

fully imitated in the Delft ware." The brilliant Kaga porcelain is almost as famous as that of Arita, while the Kudani product, with its delicate masks of enamels, is marvellously beautiful. Satsuma porcelain, the most popular of all, is known for its "soft, cream-colored tones, which have almost the effect of old ivory, with delicate color decoration broken with pale gold tints." But Kyōto is within the most easy reach of the traveller, and—largely for this reason—has become the chief centre of modern pottery manufacture. Moreover, it is famous as the home of the great artist Ninsei (seventeenth century), who ranks as the greatest potter Japan has produced, and whose specialty was the Awata faience. Chamberlain thus summarizes the other notable Japanese porcelains,—"the various kinds of Bizen ware, of which the most original are humorous figures of gods, birds, lions, and other creatures; the thin, mostly unglazed Banko ware, whose manufacturers at the present day display great ingenuity in giving quaint fanciful shapes to tea-pots and other small articles; the Awaji faience, consisting chiefly of small monochromatic pieces with a bright yellow or green glaze; the Sōma pottery, to be recognized by the picture

of a running horse; the egg-shell cups of
Mino; and the Takatori, Izumo, and Yatsu-
shiro wares, of which the latter—especially
in its more ancient specimens—are very
highly prized.''

So much, at least, has resulted from Hideyoshi's ambitious invasion of Korea. But for
him, Longfellow could never have had that
beautiful vision of Kéramos, wherein he
sings:

> Cradled and rocked in Eastern seas,
> The islands of the Japanese
> Beneath me lie; o'er lake and plain
> The stork, the heron, and the crane
> Through the clear realms of azure drift,
> And on the hillside I can see
> The villages of Imari,
> Whose thronged and flaming workshops lift
> Their twisted columns of smoke on high,
> Cloud cloisters that in ruins lie,
> With sunshine streaming through each rift,
> And broken arches of blue sky.
>
> All the bright flowers that fill the land,
> Ripple of wave on rock or sand,
> The snow on Fujiyama's cone,
> The midnight heaven so thickly sown
> With constellations of bright stars,
> The leaves that rustle, the reeds that make
> A whisper by each stream and lake,
> The saffron dawn, the sunset red,

Are painted on these lovely jars;
Again the skylark sings, again
The stork, the heron, and the crane
Float through the azure overhead,
The counterfeit and counterpart
Of Nature reproduced in art.

Iyeyasu (1542–1616) had fought under Nobunaga with Hideyoshi, and, although he had at first opposed the ambitions of his associate, the two became and re- Iyeyasu. mained firm friends. Several years before his death, Hideyoshi had given into Iyeyasu's keeping the whole of the Kwantō, comprising eight subdued but unreconstructed provinces in the very heart of eastern Hondo. The shoreline of this important territory included a great bay, at the head of which stood a fishing-village called Yedo, "the door of the bay." When presenting Iyeyasu with the munificent gift of the Kwantō, Hideyoshi advised him to make his headquarters at Yedo. He accepted this advice, and from his castle above the fishing-village dominated these turbulent provinces.

Upon the death of his friend and commander, Iyeyasu resolved to occupy his place; claiming, indeed, that this was Hideyoshi's own desire. The strong princes of the South banded in a confederacy to defeat his ambitions, and he found himself largely outnumbered.

But Iyeyasu was a veteran general of great ability, and in the battle of Sekigahara (A.D.
Battle of Sekigahara. 1600) totally overcame his opponeuts. As the battle of Shimonoseki Straits in A.D. 1185 * was the most important naval battle ever fought by the Japanese, so this proved to be the most significant land engagement in their history. "By this battle," says Dr. Griffis, "were decided the condition of Japan for over two centuries, the extinction of the claims of the line of Nobunaga and Hideyoshi, the settlement of the Tokugawa family in hereditary succession to the Shōgunate, the fate of Christianity, the isolation of Japan from the world, the fixing into permanency of the dual system and of feudalism, the glory and greatness of Yedo, and peace in Japan for two hundred and sixty-eight years."

Iyeyasu's family name of Tokugawa was
The Tokugawa Family. taken from the village of his immediate ancestors. But he was able to trace his descent to the famous Mina-

---

* See page 77.

moto clan, whose posterity had furnished Japan with her Shōguns for the last four hundred years. He was not slow to take advantage of this fact. Three years after his great battle was fought and won, he received from the Emperor the imposing title that had lain in disuse for thirty years, and founded the brilliant dynasty of the Tokugawa, which endured until Shōgunates were forever abolished upon the restoration of imperialism in 1868.

Iyeyasu signalized the beginning of a new era by establishing his capital at Yedo (now Tōkyō), just as his great progenitor, Yoritomo, had founded his power at Kamakura. His good judgment and prophetic instinct were nowhere more clearly shown than by this deed. In spite of the jeers of his critics, he foresaw the future greatness of this "door of the bay," and set an army of three hundred thousand laborers to work in the sunken marshes or upon its towering hills, grading streets and digging canals; building, indeed, for the future. His faith was justified within the next half-century, for the new capital already held a quarter million of inhabitants, and has always remained the metropolis of Japan, ranking

Founding of Tōkyō.

to-day—with its more than a million souls—
among the great cities of the world.

But the building of Yedo was only an incident in the gigantic plans of this ruler. He
Unification   brought the Shōgunate to a complex
of Empire.   perfection of which Yoritomo and
his successors had never dreamed. Building
upon the unification already achieved by Hideyoshi, he so parcelled his favors among the
great lords as to strike a perfect balance
among them, thus at one stroke bidding for
friendship and making their enmity harmless.
His three daughters he married to powerful
princes, and placed his several sons where loyalty was most sorely needed. He remained
scrupulously true to the old theory that the
Emperor was always sole ruler, and Kyōto the
only real capital; but he surrounded Kyōto
in such fashion by strong and trustworthy
princes that removal of the Emperor was
made impossible. Further, he established
easy communication between the two capitals,
building a great road to cover the distance
of over three hundred miles, with fifty-two
stations for shelter and fresh supplies of
every kind. With minute attention to detail,
he marked out the width of all roadways, set
up signs to serve as mile-posts, arranged fer-

ries, and provided laws for the regulation of society. It is doubtful whether any ruler has ever accomplished larger results in an equal space of time, or surpassed him in fertility of resources. Wherever there were two clans whose friendliness he could not buy with favors, he would quietly insert a loyal landholder between them, whose intervention effectually hindered intrigue. His ambition, unlike that of Nobunaga or Hideyoshi, was not so much for himself as for his succession. He was thoughtfully founding a dynasty. Being desirous of an abiding peace, and mindful of the avengeful feelings of Korea and China, he undid so far as possible the mischievous work of Hideyoshi by sending an embassy of friendship, who secured professions of peace in return. Then, having accomplished marvels in all directions, he was content with two brief years of the Shōgunate for himself, and—thoughtful always of the future—retired in behalf of a favorite son, so that by his own all-powerful influence he might see the succession firmly established in his family. Quietly retreating to the small city of Shizuoka at the age of sixty-three years, from his seat there he kept guard over the empire, and spent the remaining eleven years of his life in fostering the pursuit of the classics. It is the everlasting glory of this man that he laid the foundations of a peace which endured for two hundred and sixty-eight years. No other nation has a record like that; and it is all the more amazing when we recall that it ensued directly upon a millennium of bloodshed. Japan is the empire of miracles.

Under the rule of Iyeyasu, the gradually forming social structure of Japan suddenly The Class crystallized into a rigid class system System. which endures in essential principles to the present time. For convenience, we may say that there are four great social classes in Japan: "samurai," farmer, artisan, and merchant, ranking in the order named. The word "samurai" comes from an ancient verb which means "to be on guard," and was first distinctively employed with reference to the sentinels of the Emperor's palace. But, finally, "samurai" came to denote the entire warrior class, of whom the *daimyō*, or "great names," were the chief. In Japan, however, the soldier was also the scholar, the pen being companion of the sword; so that the samurai class possessed the double distinction of scholarship and bravery. The great men who wield the destinies of Japan to-day have descended, almost without exception, from the famous samurai clansmen.

Next below the warrior class came the farmers, always held in a certain respect as the sturdy tillers of the soil. When, during the peaceful Tokugawa period, the idle samurai sometimes degenerated into rowdy and dangerons swashbucklers, companies of farmers banded together into a sort of volunteer soldiery, for the especial protection of the unarmed victims of the strutting gentry.

Artisans ranked next to the farmers, and these artisans were oftentimes artists. As we have seen, Hideyoshi's generals brought back famous potters from Korea, whose Japanese disciples soon learned to excel their teachers; while the two-handed Japanese sword was wrought to a state of perfection that has scarcely been witnessed elsewhere. The farmers and artisans are creators, and therefore worthy of reverence.

But the merchant lives by exchanging the products of others, with no higher motive than money. According to a philosophy that was the exact opposite of our own sordid commercial theories, the merchants therefore

—and all who dealt merely with money—were ranked at the very bottom of the social scale.

Such were the four general classes of society. Above these classes were the *kuge,* or court nobility, who ranked in a caste above mere mortals; while at the other extreme, too low to be classed as human beings, were the despised *eta,* the outcast pariahs of Japan. These are such people as butchers or tanners, who have to do with the taking of life; and the disdain with which they are treated probably arose from the Buddhist prohibition against the slaughter of animals.

The real rulers of Japan were the *daimyō,* or chief of the samurai. These were the lords of large manors, holding their hands in fief to the Shōgun. Iyeyasu himself was simply chief of all the *daimyō,* as the name Shōgun implies; and by means of a perfected organization, radiating from him as the centre, he was able to reach every point in the circumference of his empire.

It must not be thought that the prolonged peace which he brought upon Japan impoverished the martial spirit of his people. Actual warfare is absent from the annals of the country between A.D. 1600

Turbulence.

TOMB OF THE FORTY-SEVEN RŌNIN AT TŌKYŌ.

and 1868, but the warrior-subjects never allowed their sword to lose its cunning or their spears to rust. As already intimated, many of the samurai became mere bullies and rowdies, a terror to their unarmed neighbors. It was no uncommon thing for a two-sworded dandy suddenly to draw his blade upon some poor farmer digging by the roadside, merely to try its mettle; while an occasional test of the excellence of the steel was to pile three human bodies one upon another and cleave them through at one stroke. Mr. Mitford's "Tales of Old Japan" abound in blood-curdling incidents which go to prove that Japan under Tokugawa rule was far from being a paradise of peace. The most famous of these stories is that of the "Forty-seven Rōnin." There is no space to quote it here; but the name *rōnin* is itself significant, denoting as it does the "wave-men," or wandering warriors who tossed through the country like restless billows, causing an unceasing condition of turbulence.

The government was at first friendly to foreigners, and Hideyoshi's suspicions were forgotten. "The land swarmed with Catholic friars and Catholic converts, and no embargo had yet been laid on

The First Englishman.

foreign commerce.'' But this commerce was controlled exclusively by the Portuguese and Spanish, the Dutch and English not having yet arrived upon the scene. It was during the brief rule of Iyeyasu that the first Englishman made his appearance in Japan as a resident, the same being a venturesome and shrewd-witted sailor, Will Adams. He was pilot on board the bark ''Charity,'' of the Dutch East India Company, which was wrecked off the coast of Kyūshū in the year 1600. Eight of the crew reached the shore alive, all being Dutchmen but Adams. They were kindly received and well treated in spite of the unfriendly efforts of the Portuguese. Iyeyasu being at that time in Ōsaka, Adams and one other were conveyed into his presence, and the pilot spoke a good word for the Dutch. Adams was then cast into prison, where he was kept for more than a month, expecting in due time to be killed. The Portuguese used their best offices to this end. But Adams tells us, in his quaint English, that Iyeyasu answered them and said that since ''we as yet had done to him nor to none of his lands any harm or dammage,'' it would be ''against Reason and Justice to put us to death. If our countreys had warres the one with the other, that was no cause that he should put us to death.''

The remainder of the crew became scattered, but Adams remained an inmate of Iyeyasu's castle in Yedo, where he amused himself with amateur ship-building. This fact, together with his honest and straightforward character, won him such favor with the Shōgun that he shortly found himself the possessor of a large estate, ''a living like unto a lordship in England, with eighty or ninety husbandmen, that be as my slaves or servants.'' He never returned to England, but remained twenty years in Japan, where he rendered great service to his own country and also to the Dutch, being buried at last beside his Japanese wife on his little estate near Yedo. Undoubtedly, it was due very largely to his influence that Iyeyasu's successor concluded an agreement with the Dutch, in spite of the hostile Portuguese, whereby the little kingdom of Holland received favors that gave her merchants the exclusive foreign commerce of Japan after that empire had shut its doors against the world in 1624.

Doubtless Christianity was the cause of this singular act whereby Japan became a hermit nation and remained so until Commodore Perry forced her gates just fifty years ago—that is to say, Christianity as misrepresented by its professed adherents. The favoritism shown to the Jesuits by the Pope was a continual vexation to the Franciscan and Dominican missionaries, and each party so industriously calumniated the other that it would have been wonderful had not some of their slanderous stories been at length believed by the ruling powers. This, as we have seen, was the chief cause of the incipient persecution under Hideyoshi. In Iyeyasu's time the coming of the Dutch and later of the English intensified the activity of mutual calumny, for the national enmities of the various European nations represented in Japan were at this time very marked. Every foreigner who gained the ear of Iyeyasu or of his son the Shōgun would abuse other foreigners, the Dutch and English warring against the insidious designs of the Jesuits, while the Portuguese berated the Spanish, and both of these united in violent abuse of the Teutons. All parties were variously to blame. Anjirō had said to Xavier, when first they met, that his people would not immediately

Christian Dissensions.

consent to Christianity, but would willingly investigate its claims, and above all would observe as to whether or not the Christians practised what they preached,—"whether conduct agreed with words." What happened? When the Roman Catholics became established in Kyūshū, they preached the "gospel of peace" by fierce persecutions of the Buddhists.* The Portuguese "Christian" merchants sold thousands of helpless Japanese into slavery,—"slaves became so cheap that even the Malay and negro servants of the Portuguese speculated in the bodies of Japanese slaves, who were bought and sold and transported."† Nor were the Dutch by any means blameless. The immense disparity between the creed of Christians and their actual deeds must have begotten in the minds of patriotic Japanese a profound distrust of foreigners. At any rate, Iyeyasu, who at first had seemed friendly enough towards the Christians, gradually became so prejudiced against them that in his "legacy," or will, he recommended

---

* Murray's " Japan," pages 241, 242. " Mikado's Empire," Griffis, Book I., page 253.

† " Mikado's Empire," Griffis, Book I., page 254.

universal religious toleration, with a single significant exception. "High and low," he says, "may alike follow their own inclinations with respect to religious tenets which have obtained down to the present time, except as regards the false and corrupt school (known as Christianity)."

So early as 1606 he issued his first warning on the subject,—for albeit in nominal retire-

Christian Persecutions. ment, he remained the real ruler of the empire. Recalling Hideyoshi's decree, he noted with regret that many of his subjects persisted in the Christian faith, which he advised them, for the good of the state, to renounce and forsake at once. But the Catholic citizens of Nagasaki, under the leadership of foreign priests, showed their contempt for such warnings a few years later, by a spectacular celebration in honor of the founder of the Jesuits, Ignatius Loyola; while a similar jubilee took place in the neighboring principality of Arima, whose *daimyō* was a zealot of the faith. This was in direct violation of a law which forbade precisely such displays. Naturally, Iyeyasu was enraged, especially when he discovered, as he supposed (A.D. 1611), the existence of a conspiracy among foreign and Japanese

Christians, directed against the sovereignty of the empire. Perfecting his plans, he issued in 1614 a decree that commanded the members of all Christian orders to leave Japan, all Christian churches to be demolished, and all converts to be compelled to recant. Christianity being strongest in Kyūshū, as many as ten thousand troops were despatched thither in order to prevent any revolt. But so bold were the Catholic princes, that in this very year the *daimyō* of a northern principality sent an embassy to the Pope and to the King of Spain, praying for the coming of more missionaries.

The edict was rigorously enforced in Kyūshū. Churches were demolished and hundreds of missionaries deported, while the persecutions of the native Christians are reported to have been ''beyond description horrible.''

Iyeyasu's anger was finally wrought to its utmost heat by discovering that the Jesuits were paying significant court to Hideyori, the son of Hideyoshi, in his lordly castle at Ōsaka. The survival of this princely heir of an older rule, which still had its fervent admirers, seemed to threaten the dearest ambitions of the Tokugawa, especially in view of the ardor with which the Christians were espousing his cause. With characteristic decisiveness of action, the aged Iyeyasu at once declared battle against the youthful heir of the Taikō, shut up in his castle at Ōsaka. After a protracted siege, a battle was fought in June, 1615, resulting in the death of Hideyori and his mother, with the destruction of the citadel, and the complete overthrow of the political power of the Christians. The Jesuit histories say that a hundred thousand soldiers perished in this conflict, and that it was bloodier than any of the terrible preceding wars.

Iyeyasu died in the following year, but his son continued the persecutions with a still more vehement fury. A learned student of the period * has graphically described this Japanese reign of terror, which recalls the utmost cruelties of the early martyrdoms in Rome. "We read of Christians being executed in a barbarous manner in sight of each other, of their being hurled from the tops of precipices, of their being burned alive, of their being torn asunder by oxen, of their

The Reign of Terror.

---

* Mr. J. H. Gubbins in Asiatic Society Transactions. Quoted by Murray.

IYEYASU'S TOMB AT NIKKÔ.

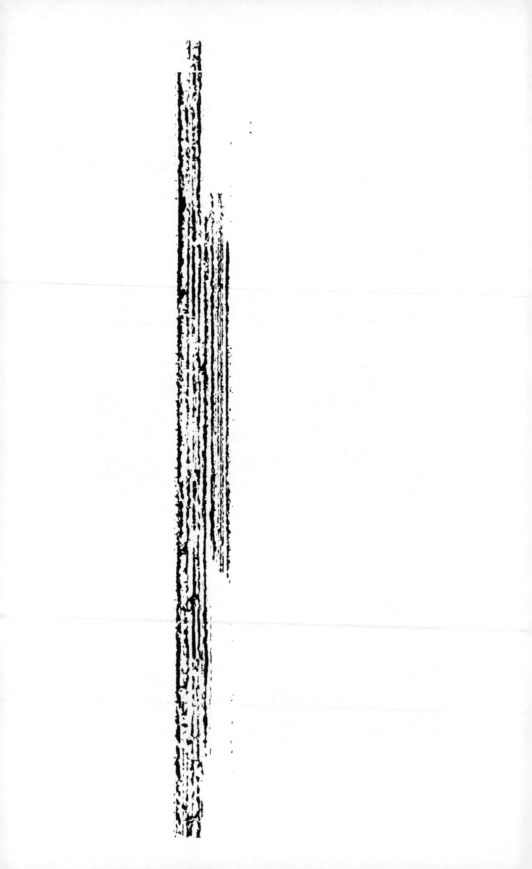

being tied up in rice-bags, which were heaped up together, and of the pile thus formed being set on fire. Others were tortured before death by the insertion of sharp spikes under the nails of their hands and feet, while some poor wretches, by a refinement of horrid cruelty, were shut up in cages and there left to starve with food before their eyes. Let it not be supposed that we have drawn on the Jesuit accounts solely for this information. An examination of the Japanese records will show that the case is not overstated." And Dr. Griffis adds: "All the tortures that barbaric hatred or refined cruelty could invent were used to turn thousands of their fellow-men into carcases and ashes. Yet few of the natives quailed or renounced their faith. They calmly let the fire of wood cleft from the crosses before which they once prayed consume them, or walked cheerfully to the blood-pit, or were flung alive into the open grave about to be filled up. Mothers carried their babes at their bosoms, or their children in their arms to the fire, the sword, or the precipice's edge, rather than leave them behind to be educated in the pagan faith. If any one doubt the sincerity and fervor of the Christian converts of to-day, or the ability of the Japanese to accept a higher form of faith, or their willingness to suffer for what they believe, they have but to read the accounts preserved in English, Dutch, French, Latin, and Japanese, of various witnesses to the fortitude of the Japanese Christians of the seventeenth century. The annals of the primitive Church furnish no instances of sacrifice or heroic constancy, in the Coliseum or the Roman arenas, that were not paralleled on the dry river-beds and execution-grounds of Japan.''

In 1623 Iyeyasu's grandson acceded to the Shōgunate — Iyemitsu — destined to become

Iyemitsu.

the next greatest ruler of the line. He relented none of the terrors of the persecution, but devised and encouraged óthers. For example, the Christians in that part of Kyūshū where hot springs abound were plunged into the scalding water or suffocated in the sulphurous fumes until they were perishing from weakness, when their sufferings were relaxed so that they might be victimized repeatedly. A refinement of this particular form of persecution provided that the martyr's back should be gashed with swords and the steaming water dashed directly upon the raw flesh. "Other cases are recorded too horrible to be related, and which only the ingenuity of hell could have devised.''

It was at this time that the ceremony of ''trampling on the cross'' was invented. Little slabs of wood or of brass were used, — one of which the writer has examined,—bearing a rough image of a crucifix. An official inquisitor was appointed, and on a set day in every year each household in the neighborhood of Nagasaki would be invaded, and every inmate required to trample on the cross. In cases of refusal, the Christian thus apprehended would be given over to the executioners of the inquisition.

"Trampling on the Cross."

But for all this, Christianity could not be exterminated. The tenacity with which the believers held to their faith is strikingly proved by the fact that when the Shimabara Rebellion occurred in 1637, some thirty thousand Christians took part in it. The immediate occasion of the insurrection was the inhuman cruelty of a *daimyō* towards his tenants; but the persecuted Christians, driven to desperation by so many years of suffering, seized the opportunity to join the farmers and make common

The Shimabara Massacre.

war for their rights. Iyemitsu sent a hundred and sixty thousand seasoned troops against this desperate but untutored company, so that the pitiful story is soon told. The thirty thousand victims of oppression found themselves beleaguered in a deserted castle, where for a hundred and two days they defied assault. The Dutch traders at Nagasaki are said to have furnished cannoury against them. When the castle at length fell, on the 12th of April, 1638, every man, woman, and child was put to death, and general persecutions were renewed with such vigor that Christianity now seemed annihilated. We read that above the door of the deserted castle the following legend was inscribed on stone: "So long as the sun shall warm the earth, let no Christian be so bold as to come to Japan; and let all know that the King of Spain himself, or the Christian's God, or the Great God of all, if he violate this command, shall pay for it with his head." A special body of police, known as "The Christian Inquiry," was permanently organized, who, in connection with the Buddhist priesthood, kept the closest lookout for Christians. Large sign-boards were placed in every village, which warned against the hated faith with heavy penalties. And by action which Iyemitsu had taken in 1624, all Europeans were banished utterly from the empire, so that Christianity never could enter again. The only apparent exception was not an exception at all, for the Dutch traders were shut up on a tiny island in Nagasaki harbor,—Deshima,—and The Dutch. rigidly prevented from entrance on the mainland. Only two ships could come from Holland in a year, and once annually the traders had to pay costly tribute to Yedo. Dr. Cary tells us that there were two reasons why the Dutch were allowed even these privileges: first, because the government considered that it owed to them the discovery of the Jesuit plots, one of their captains claiming to have intercepted a letter to the King of Portugal asking for troops to effect a revolution; and, secondly, because the Dutch carefully abstained from all profession of Christianity, as acknowledged by their own historian, Kaempfer. One of them, being taxed with his belief, replied, ''No, I am not a Christian; I am a Dutchman.'' It is said that they even consented to trample on the cross.

So it was that Japan put up her bars, and remained for two hundred and thirty years a hermit nation. There are no events to record, simply because nothing happened. The Hermit Nation. It was a season of mysterious silence, a dull winter of preparation for a dazzling spring, a prolonged period of adolescence during which those forces were slowly maturing that made ''young Japan'' ready for the lessons of manhood when America broke down the bars. To trace in some slight fashion the quiet growth of these forces will complete our study of Japanese ''childhood.''

THE late John Fiske was the author of a most interesting theory of childhood. He claimed that the prolonged period of human infancy accounts to a great degree for our mental supe- *The Real Meaning of Childhood.* riority to the brutes. Childhood means preparation. A little wolf can take care of itself when only a few days old, whereas a little child is the most helpless thing in the world, and remains so for years. But this helplessness, with the resultant care that it secures from the parents, gives the child opportunity for pure growth. Throughout the long period of protected infancy, the nerve-cells are stored with a largess of power that makes for strong manhood. This fact of a lengthened infancy, the evolutionists assure us, is one of the greatest boons of the race.

Whether this interesting theory be true or not, it serves as an apt illustration of what took place in Japan. There can be little doubt that the causes of the amazing progress that Japan has made in the last fifty years came to their full maturity in the long silent season that preceded: that reign of profound peace and of eremite seclusion beginning with the Tokugawa Shōgunate and continuing two hundred and sixty-eight years, or until Perry came from the West. This gave opportunity for the dim traits of the race to become ineffaceably deepened,—for those vague lineaments that had begun to form in the womb of the turbulent past to become the fixed features of manhood. The middle ages in Europe have long been recognized as the matrix of modern civilization, the formative period of the present; but this is true to a far greater extent of Japan. The Tokugawa age, in particular, was her season of character building, the educative age of her childhood.

The influences of this period so wrought upon and developed the inchoate national tendencies as to produce five fundamental perfected qualities that account in large measure for the wondrous Japan of to-day. These attributes are bravery, loyalty, thoroughness, alertness, and self-control. The first two are qualities of the heart, the next two pertain to the

Five Fundamental Qualities.

mind, while the last means the schooling of the will. It may be worth while to consider briefly the manner in which this threefold culture came to be.

Bravery has always been the chief ideal of Japanese character. What beauty meant to the Greeks, and right to the Romans, and purity to the Hebrews of *Bravery.* old, bravery has meant to Japan. A man may be whatever else he pleases, but if he only be brave, he keeps the respect of his fellows, and may even become a demigod. An old proverb runs, "Among flowers, the cherry; among men, the warrior." Every one knows that the cherry-blossom is queen in the "Flowery Kingdom;" so is the soldier the king among men. In the middle ages, the development of bravery was undertaken with deliberate system; and in the schools of the Tokugawa period martial exercises were made a part of the daily curriculum. This was of a kind far different from the training in the military schools of the West; with us our soldier-work is play, but in Japan it was earnest to the death. The highest test of physical courage is the willingness to yield one's own life; and the institution of *hara-kiri* was drilled into the very marrow of the nation. The young men at school "went through again and again the tragic details of the commission of *harakiri*, and had it impressed on their youthful imaginations with such force and vividness that when the time for its actual enactment came, they were able to meet the bloody reality without a tremor and with perfect composure." Even the women were taught the equivalent duty of *jigai*,—that is to say, "piercing the throat with a dagger so as to sever the arteries by a single thrust-and-cut movement." The samurai maiden in service was bound by loyalty to her mistress not less closely than the warrior to the lord; and the heroines of Japanese feudalism were many. Judged from the ethical point of view, suicide is the most cowardly of crimes. But the Japanese, blind to the moral aspect of the deed, have exalted it into a virtue because it tests physical bravery. And the elaboration of suicide into a national institution, practised and belauded for centuries, has doubtless done more than anything else to make the Japanese soldier so daring.*

* Mr. Mitford, in the Appendix of his "Tales of Old Japan," has given a most graphic and impressive account of this remarkable ceremony and its effects.

Next to bravery itself, the quality which the Japanese most highly prize is patriotic loyalty. The roots of this virtue were traced in the first part of this book to Loyalty. the religious tenets of filialism. In Oriental usage, the term "father" is so broad as to include any superior, and the obligation of filial piety becomes the more intense as the authority ascends. In the schooling period of Japan, the retainer was taught loyalty to his *daimyō* by the most heroic methods. For example, upon the death of his lord, he was to be ready for a living burial for himself, only his head remaining above ground, while he was left to starve slowly to death, and that without murmuring. Many a heroic retainer endured this supreme test of loyalty. Kusunoki, one of Go-Daigo's generals, and a paragon of Japanese patriotism, prayed for seven lives that he might give them all to his master. Iyeyasu and his followers succeeded in binding the *daimyō* to the Shōgun as the retainer was bound to the *daimyō*, and thus Japan was welded into a unity such as few countries have seen. Iyemitsu compelled all of the *daimyō* to live at the capital during six months of the year, and to leave their wives and families there

for the other half. The *daimyō* took oath
to be obedient to his orders, sealing the
pledge with their blood. He assumed the
additional title of Tai Kun ("tycoon"),
meaning "great prince," and it was retained by all of his successors. But the
loyalty of retainer and *daimyō* and Shōgun
alike was ultimately centred in the Emperor. Although his rule seemed often
enough to be no more than a name, yet his
"heavenly descent" and the mysterious se-
elusion that veiled him appealed powerfully
to the sentiment of the people, who have ever
held him in awe. Thus there resulted a unified organism of government, based upon an
ever centralizing loyalty, which endures essentially to this day, and gives Japan a power
out of all proportion to mere size. The Emperor is the soul of the realm, to which the
whole body does reverence; the Shōgunate
(now supplanted by the clan ministry) being
the brain, while the masses furnish the brawn.
Loyalty is the life-principle that binds all
into a common whole, for loyalty is even the
law of the Emperor, who worships his own
ancestors.

`The Tokugawa period provided full oppor-
tunity for drill in the habit of thoroughness.

Iyeyasu set an example in the study of the
·Chinese classics that was eagerly emulated
by posterity. So ingrained has
Chinese become in the literary   Thoroughness.
language of Japan that no one can mas-
ter the latter who does not know also the
former. Consequently, a Japanese school-
boy does not learn to "read" until he is
sixteen or seventeen years of age, because
of the immense multiplicity and complexity
of the Chinese ideographs. That is to say,
where an American school-boy has to learn
an alphabet of only twenty-six simple letters, the Japanese school-boy must master
at least five thousand out of a total of sixty
thousand ideographs, most of which are exceedingly complex, and many of which are
differentiated only in the minutest particu-
lars. But consider what this means towards
thoroughness. Poring over these "Chinese
puzzles" for generations has had the effect
of emphasizing the native tendency of attention to detail until thoroughness has become
a most marked characteristic. Coupled with
an inherent esthetic, which the Tokugawa influences fostered into exquisite taste; and
linked with the Oriental habit of patient industry, Japanese thoroughness has produced

the most minutely perfect specimens of art
that have ever delighted the world. An artist will chisel at a little block of ivory for
years,—not to reap pecuniary reward, but to
satisfy his passion towards perfection,—until
at length you hold in your hands a tiny figure
which is a microcosm in itself, and will yield
to the microscope alone the completeness of
its dainty perfections. The same is true of
cloisonné work, and of the exquisite productions in lacquer.* I have before me as I
write a napkin-ring of Kyōto *cloisonné* that
is less than two inches in diameter, with a
band not quite an inch wide, upon which I
have counted seventy-eight separate designs,
made in twenty shades of color, and from

---

* " Need it be explained that cloisonné is a species of
mosaic, whose characteristic feature is a thin net-work
of copper or brass soldered on to a foundation of solid
metal, the interstices or cells of the net-work—the
cloisons, as they are technically called—being then filled
in with enamel paste of various colors, and the process
completed by several bakings, rubbings, and polish-
ings, until the surface becomes as smooth as it is hard?
. . . with a wealth of ornament, an accuracy of design,
a harmony of color, that are simply miraculous when
one considers the character of the material employed
and the risks to which it is subjected in the process of
manufacture."—CHAMBERLAIN, " Things Japanese."

CLOISONNÉ ARTISTS AT WORK.
Inlaying the decorative outlines.

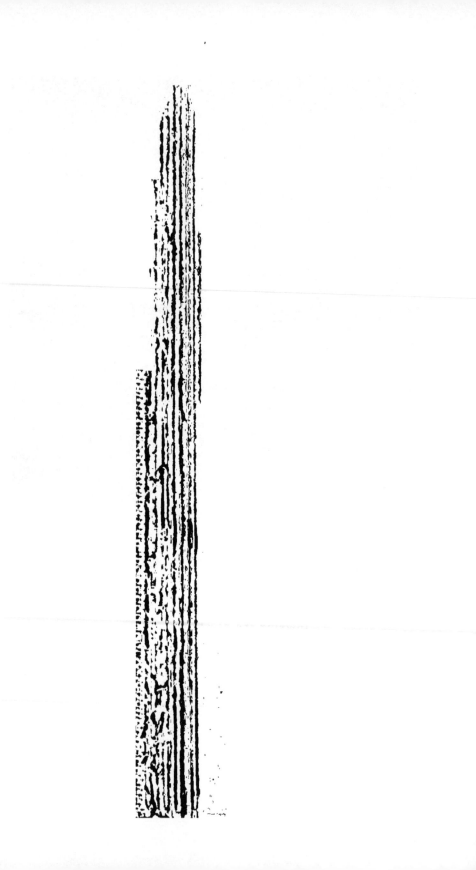

at least four hundred pieces of metal. It is an object-lesson in Japanese thoroughness.

Now, it used to be said by critics, that while the Japanese are thorough in minutiæ, they lack the capacity for thoroughness in things that are really worth while. It was pointed out that while producing ivory carvings at home, they had to send abroad for their battleships. But the critics were in too great a hurry. You cannot build battleships without a shipyard. The nation now has its docks and ship factories at Yokosuka, where, in an amazingly short space of time, Japanese officers have so emulated the example of Peter the Great of Russia that now the Japanese are beginning to build vessels that vie with those of any nation in the world.

If any additional proof were needed of Japanese thoroughness, it has certainly been furnished in the course of the great war with Russia. With a foresight that overlooked nothing, and with an attentiveness that scrutinized everything, they planned and executed a campaign which for sheer thoroughness has never been surpassed in human history. Doubtless the school in which they

perfected this priceless habit was the seclu-
sive session of the Tokugawa.

A mental quality which is the complement
of thoroughness is the equally valuable habit

Alertness.
of alertness. This also was taught
to an already nimble race until they
have become a nation of "prestidigitators."
Sleight-of-hand is nothing but a dexterity so
rapid that the movements are lost by the eye,
resulting in effects that had no visible cause.
For the last fifty years, Japan has played
the rôle of magician, while the audience of
nations has gazed open-mouthed at this mar-
vellons handling of great implements whereof
the little land had but now been altogether
ignorant. As Lafcadio Hearn suggests,
Japan has been playing *jiū-jutsu* with the
complex civilization of the West. This is
an art, or a science, which grew out of the
silence of those hermit-days when Japan was
developing her peculiar genius to perfection.
It is occult, but its mystery is the mystery
of swiftness coupled with scientific skill.
That is to say, *jiū-jutsu* is embodied alertness. The first time I saw it practised was
on the grounds of our old college campus,
where we had two or three Japanese students. One of them was standing one day

at a ball-game, when a great strapping student from the backwoods came clumsily and threw him on the ground. The dapper little man arose smiling, flicked off the dust from his clothes, and quietly bided his time. No one foresaw what was coming. He waited until the big bundle of brawn stood lost in contemplation of the game, then he came swiftly behind him and with just a flash, just a touch that was nothing—there sprawled his great foe on the ground! We who saw it were mystified, but the big victim was most mystified of all. He had felt nothing until he felt the ground. Later on I witnessed private exhibitions in Japan, but came away hardly the wiser. It is remarkable skill in anatomy joined with marvellous agility,—it is not strength, but softness and swiftness,—it uses the strength of the foe as the strongest weapon against him,—its name calls it "the science of gentleness." Experts in *jiū-jutsu* appear to achieve the miraculous. There lies a stalwart antagonist with a bone broken, a great tendon strained, or even in a state of suspended animation: how was it done? Not by force, but by swift softness. He was lured on to overreach himself, until there was a sudden invisible nimble flash, and it was over.

But there is no need to write further, for has not Japan played *jiū-jutsu* with Russia while all the world wondered? The chief secret of her brilliant campaign is in her astounding alertness, which is a marked characteristic of the race. For quick receptiveness and rapid assimilation of mental food they are without parallel in the history of the world; the will springing out into action as soon as the concept is formed. "The race is not always to the swift, nor the battle to the brave;" but Japan combines the boldness of the lion with the swiftness of the deer.

It is of no use to school the heart and the mind, however, unless the will also be trained.

Self-Control. The most important lesson that it can learn is self-control. And let it be remembered that Buddhism, with all of its errors, brought this greatly needed lesson to Japan. The Japanese by nature is intensely individual,—impatient of restraint, impetuous, restive, headlong,—eager to live his own life in his own way, to fulfil the mission of the individual, heedless of the welfare of the race. Buddhism came and laid its soothing hand upon him. It bade him be still, to repress his desires, to seek his Nirvana in extinction, to lose his one life in the All. The Japanese has never been a thorough convert to Buddhism, simply because it contradicts his nature. But by an age-long familiarity with its teachings, which were drilled into his mind from early childhood, he received from this great religion of repression precisely the will-discipline he needed. Unlike the phlegmatic Chinese, his impassiveness is not innate, but acquired. "Childhood" under the tutorship of Buddhism has enabled him to bridle his fiery will in such fashion that he guides it in what direction he pleases. When at length he came out from his seclusion suddenly into the dazzling arena, it was to this Buddhistic schooling of the will that he owed the strength so to restrain himself from surprise, and so to direct his wonderfully developed powers of mind and heart as to become the modern wonder of the world.

I would have my purpose clearly understood. I have not attempted to write in general of Japanese traits,—that has already been done.* And I do not present the Japanese character as ideal. Before we have

---

* See the chapter with this heading in "Japan To-Day."

finished this book we shall see its gross faults, its vast needs. I have simply come with an open mind to a study of the "childhood" age of Japan, and it has seemed to me that the peculiar influences of that most peculiar period tended especially to develop towards perfection the qualities of bravery, loyalty, thoroughness, alertness, and self-control. Long experience in living among the people confirms this judgment. And I believe that it is the remarkable combination of these five great attributes of national character that has enabled Japan to accomplish the seemingly impossible, and become a great world-power in a day.

The serious depths of the Japanese character are often concealed from superficial *National Pastimes.* observers by an ever-present surface of gayety. In the opening pages of this book I have called the country an overgrown playground. So far as outward appearances are concerned, the expression is literally true. The older folk, when indoors, amuse themselves constantly with diversions similar to checkers and chess; nor do they fail to take active part in the almost innumerable festivals. Much of the time is spent out of doors, in quest of literal "re-creation;" for

A HOLIDAY IN AN IRIS GARDEN.

doubtless a great deal of the freshness and alertness of the Japanese brain comes from the fact that it constantly creates itself anew from contact with nutritious nature. It is a gentle kind of play, however, having extremely little place for athletics, but much for leisurely conviviality. The theatre is extensively patronized, and a single performance will sometimes continue for days in succession. The audience supply themselves with luncheons, and return home for a night's sleep between the acts!

During the silent years of the secluded national "childhood," the games of childhood were not overlooked in the pursuit of more serious issues. New-year espe-cially was always a time of festivity, and continues to be the great holiday season of new Japan. A game in which the girls always indulge at this time is a picturesque version of battledoor and shuttlecock, played in the open streets. Clad in their brightest garments, with faces powdered and lips painted "until they resemble the peculiar colors seen on a beetle's wings," they play in brilliant groups, tossing a shuttlecock made of a round gilded seed, ornamented with bright feathers arranged like the petals of a flower. The

Children's Games.

11

battledoor, made of wood, bears upon one side the carved image of some hero or heroine or famous belle. The girls are said to be especially fond of this game, because it affords such excellent opportunity for the display of personal beauty. While they toss the gilded shuttlecock to and fro, their teasing brothers sing a song to the wind that it may blow and spoil the game, while the girls themselves sing a counter-petition in favor of calm breezes for their favorite out-of-door sport.

But the winds blow strong in the month of March, and then the boys have such fine fun with kites as can be found nowhere else in the world. They are of all sizes and shapes, some being six feet square. The traveller is often startled as a chance glance skyward will suddenly show him a great floating monster silhouetted vividly on the surface of the blue upper sea. A favorite diversion is to paint two kites with the faces of rival warriors, and cause them to duel in mid-air. A tense splinter of whalebone, set in at the top of the frame, utters the most blood-curdling howls as it vibrates in the wind; while the cords which tether the two duellists are stuccoed for several feet of their topmost length with powdered glass, so that they saw up and down against each other until one or the other kite falls to the ground, to become the captive of the victor.

Thus even the games are employed to increase the martial spirit of the children. Most famous of the sports of this sort are the "Hundred Tales" and the notable "Trial of Pluck." The latter game is surely well named. In the daytime a company of boys will prepare for the trial by planting a number of flags in lonely places, such as graveyards, or in the darkest hollows of the nearest haunted valley. Then, night being come, they assemble and recount the most awful tales of horror they can think of, requiring all of their number to go singly by turns, after each story, and bring back a flag to prove pluck. The "Hundred Tales" is an in-door variation of the "Test of Pluck," and may be played by boys and girls together of a winter evening. In a distant lonesome chamber there burns a dim oil lamp having a wick of a hundred separate threads. The party sit down around the brazier in one of the living-rooms of the household, while some expert grown-up story-teller recounts one by one a hundred gruesome stories. After each tale is told, the children must go by turns, and singly, to bring back through the darkness a thread from the eerie lamp. As strand after strand is removed, the light becomes dimmer and more mysterious, until the child on whom falls the unlucky lot of removing the hundredth thread almost always sees some huge imagined nightmare of terror.

Nowadays, foreign sports are making headway in the schools, much to the improvement of the Japanese physique. Baseball is the most popular of all, and the stranger some day discovers that the loud cry of the queer word "Ow-toe!" which continually resounds on the diamond, is simply the japanned form of our "out." One day I heard the captain of a steam-launch give his engineer the mysterious shouted order, "O-rai-go-haid!" and discovered that the steamboat lingo is in this case a revised edition of our commonplace, "All right, go ahead!"

The great play-seasons of the year, next to New-year, are the times of the various festivals in the towns and cities.

Festival Shows.

In the old Southern city of Saga I went one night with a company of Japanese school-boys to what might be called the circus portion of the fair-ground, and was well repaid for the visit. In the menagerie department of the circus, the star attraction proved to be a meek and long-suffering sheep, surrounded by an open-mouthed company of admirers. He had been duly caged and chained, being placarded as a very dangerous animal from the West. Sheep do not thrive in Japan, and as this was the first native-born American I had met for many months, a fellow-feeling made me wondrous kind. For, to tell the whole truth, I was made to feel sheepish myself, since I easily divided honors with the ruminating ram as a curious stranger from the unknown land across the rolling sea.

There was plenty to surprise me, however, in the "side shows." Here, for example, sat a dainty little girl upon the floor, while a great hairy Ainu from the North leaped in an ever-narrowing circle around her, yelling like mad, and brandishing an ugly double-edged sword, until finally he sliced off her head. It apparently toppled over, while the curtain went down, to ascend an instant later and show us the dead head on a table, with nothing whatever underneath. The curtain flew down once more and as quickly ascended, when, presto! there sat the same smiling little girl, ready to have her head sliced off again.

But the creature that fascinated me absolutely, so that I had difficulty in tearing myself away from the creepy thing, was called by my companions "the neck-stretcher." It was a woman, seated on a platform above the audience, and smoking a tiny pipe, after the fashion prevailing in Japan. Presently she began to turn her head from side to side, very slowly, while her neck grew ever longer and thinner, until at the last it was about a yard long, and no bigger than the neck of a goose. Then this accomplished lady, always reaching up to her ascended mouth and smoking, placidly closed her eyes and screwed her head down into its place again. How was it done? Ah, but that is another story.

Let us return from this glimpse at the playground to trace the growth of classical education in Japan's period of " childhood." As noted in the opening pages, Buddhism was the earliest patron of Japanese learning. With the great name of Shōtoku Taishi * must be ranked the monk Kōbō Daishi (A.D. 774–835). Famous as a scholar in Pali, Sanscrit, and Chinese, his chief distinction consists in the invention of

Buddhistic Education.

---

* See page 56.

the Japanese syllabary. This was an attempt to simplify the written language by the substitution of an "alphabet" of only forty-seven characters for the sixty thousand Chinese ideographs. It was a most noteworthy and laudable endeavor, but can hardly be called a complete success. For there are now two forms of these characters, "square" and "flowing," which must be learned in addition to the ideographs by one who would know native literature. It must not be forgotten, however, that the invention was of great benefit to the ignorant, who may at least learn to read and write the simple "kana." Thus this Buddhist monk may properly be called the first great friend of popular education in Japan, who richly deserves his posthumous name of Kōbō Daishi, which signifies, "the Great Teacher spreading abroad the Law." This name was conferred by the exiled Emperor Go-Daigo, a hundred years after the monk's death, his original name being Kūkai.

But the patron god of Japanese letters is the saint known and worshipped as Tenjin (heavenly god), who when living bore the name of Michizane (died A.D. 903). Coming into prominence as the teacher of a future emperor, he eventually became the counsellor of the great Daigo, who through his influence became not only a patron of letters, but— as we have seen—the sole mediæval emperor strong enough to rule alone. Michizane was one of the greatest scholars of his age, besides being the author of various historical works. But his political power brought him into disfavor with those who wished to control the court, and he was therefore banished to Kyūshū. Here he used to ride about on a cow, and a recumbent image of his favorite animal frequently adorns the temples where he is worshipped. The most notable of these is the *Kame-ido* in Tōkyō, famous also for its spring-time beauty of wistaria blossoms. (See the frontispiece.) His annual festival occurs on the twenty-fifth day of June, and the twenty-fifth day of every month is devoted to his memory in the schools. School-children still pray to this patron saint of scholarship to give them success with their books.

The arts that were fostered by Buddhism not only reached a very high degree of perfection, but were also diffused throughout the nation as during no other period, under the friendly in-

Buddhism and Artistic Culture.

fluences of the long peaceful rule of the Tokugawa family. It then came to pass that every
household utensil, even the most trifling ob-
jcet, was in respect of design an object of
art. "Even such articles of common use as
a bronze candlestick, a brass lamp, an iron
kettle, a paper lantern, a bamboo curtain, a
wooden pillow, a wooden tray, will reveal to
educated eyes a sense of beauty and fitness
entirely unknown to Western cheap produc-
tion. Then also was developed the art of
illustration; then came into existence those
wonderful color-prints (the most beautiful
made in any age or country) which are now
so eagerly collected by wealthy dilettanti."

But it was especially the arts of carving
and of lacquer-work that came to their highest fruition at this period. The
Buddhist temples at Nikkō, me-   Wood-Carving.
morials of Iyeyasu and Iyemitsu, are especially lavish in artistic adornment. There
may be seen three wooden figures from the
hand of Hidari Jingorō, or Jingorō "the left-
handed" (A.D. 1594–1634) that rank among
the chief art treasures of the world—for
their creator has been styled "the Japanese
Phidias." One of these three figures is a
marvellous sleeping cat, wherein the artist

has achieved the extremely difficult feat of setting forth in unresponsive wood the "fine and very delicate distinction between death and sleeping life." Many legends attest his almost superhuman skill, and his influence may still be seen in those dainty ivory carvings that have made the disciples of his craft famous throughout the world.

Another wood-carver of immortal greatness belonged to this same seventeenth century—Ogawa Ritsuwo by name.

Lacquer-Work.

But he derives distinctive pre-eminence from his skill in lacquer-work, which has been called the noblest of Japanese crafts. In the Tokugawa period this hitherto somewhat crude branch of industry sprang rapidly into a very extensive development. Nearly every *daimyō* then had his court lacquerer, Dr. Griffis informs us, and a set of lacquered furniture was an essential possession of every noble lady. "On the birth of a daughter, it was common for the lacquer artist to begin the making of a mirror-case, a washing-bowl, a cabinet, a clothes-rack, or a chest of drawers, often occupying from one to five years on a single article. An *inrō*, or pill-box, might require several years of perfection, though small enough to go into a

"THE SLEEPING CAT."
A famous wood-carving by Hidari Jingorō.

fob. By the time the young lady was marriageable, her outfit of lacquer was superb.'' Hartmann gives us the following brief account of this industry: ''The Japanese lacquer varnish is gathered from the *urushi*-tree, which, it is said, supplies a finer gum than that of any other species. It is subjected to various manipulations and refining processes before it can safely be mixed with coloring matter. From the first gathering to the last application, increasing care as to the dryness or moisture of the atmosphere, the exclusion of every particle of dust, and other conditions, are essential. The workmen are 'in possession of secret processes,' and we must be satisfied with knowing that layer after layer—up to fifty coats—of the lacquer varnish are laid on the basic material at intervals of days or weeks, and that after it has thoroughly dried—and, by a strange paradox, it must dry in dampness, well moistened, or even saturated with water, else it will run or stick—the same smoothing process with lumps of charcoal and the fingers, after all the most perfect polishing instruments, is repeated. The articles to be lacquered are generally made of fine-grained pine wood, very carefully seasoned and smoothed, so that not

the slightest inequality of surface or roughness of edge remains. But also silk, ivory,
and tortoise-shell are used. In the finer and
older specimens, bringing their weight in
gold, the varnish is so hard and immune that
neither boiling water nor boiling oil will affect
its surface." This should be cleaned, however, only with a fine silk cloth. We are told
that some of the finest collections in Europe
have been ruined by the use of a common
feather-duster.

The Buddhist temples of the Tokugawa
period not only abound in exquisite carving
and lacquer-work, but also afford the highest
examples of the development of Japanese
architecture. More accurately speaking, the
Buddhism and development of the strictly native
Architecture. architecture is to be seen in the
simple Shintō temples, with their peculiar ex-
terior ridge-poles held down by cigar-shaped
cross-beams at either end, and the invariable
graceful *torii* in front—these peculiar gateways having been anciently built as perches
for the sacred birds; but in the Buddhist
temple the Japanese have once more taken
up a foreign form and made it peculiarly
their own. "In the Buddhist temples the
marvellous instinct of the Japanese for

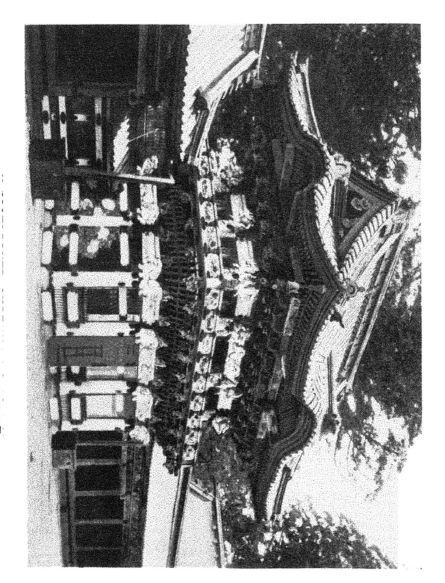

A SCULPTURED GATEWAY AT NIKKŌ

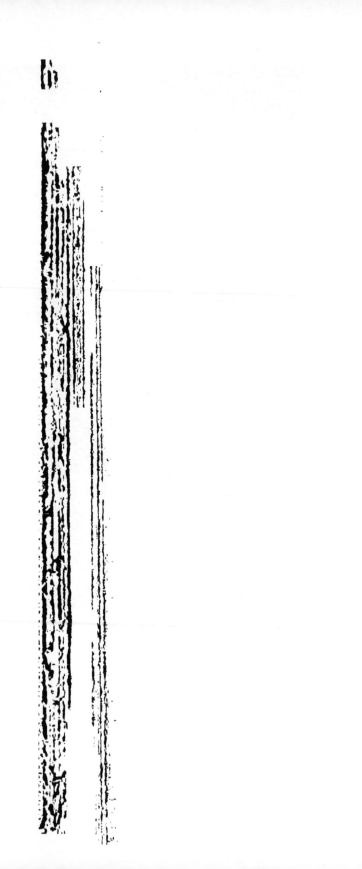

grouping and color has had full sway. The first building in a Buddhist shrine which asserts itself is the *sammon*, or two-storied gateway, resembling in the distribution of its upper story the 'gates of extensive wisdom,' etc., in the noble official residences of Korea. The framing of the lower story, however, is arranged so as to form niches, in which stand frequently the God of Thunder and the Wind Deity, the face of one being always painted a livid green, that of the other a deep vermilion, as though congested. Passing through the *sammon* the visitor finds himself in the first terraced court, only to encounter another gateway, more imposing than the last, leading to a second court, and so on to a third, until by traversing terrace after terrace he at length reaches the oratory and chapel. These court-yards are usually filled with all the concomitant buildings of the Buddhist cult, as well as with a number of bronze and stone lanterns presented by the *daimyōs* in token of repentance for past sins. Belfries, priests' apartments, a *rinzo*, or revolving library, a kitchen, a treasure-house, a pavilion containing the holy-water cistern, and pagodas rise on either hand throughout, all crowned with festooned roofs, beautifully carved and lacquered, embellished with statuary, and covered with ornaments in wood, bronze, and ivory, representing gods, dragons, birds, lions, tapirs, unicorns, elephants, tigers, flowers, and plants,—in fact, every symbol known to the Japanese, whether original, or borrowed from the Chinese or Koreans. Among the most important of the supplementary buildings are the pagodas, which are invariably square, like those of Korea. They are usually divided into five or seven stories, each set a little within the one below, and girt about with balconies and overhanging eaves, as in China. The whole is usually lacquered in dull red, save the lowest story, on which a bewildering mass of painted carvings distracts the eye, while high above all a twisted spire of bronze forms the culmination.''

We are told that when Dr. Dresser, author of ''Art and Art Industries in Japan,'' was studying the temple architecture of the country, he noted with surprise an apparent waste of material in the magnificent pagoda at Nikkō. ''He did not understand why an enormous log of wood ascended in the centre of the structure from its base to the apex. This mass of

Architecture and Earthquakes.

timber, he tells us, is nearly two feet in diameter, and near the lower end a log equally large is bolted to each of the four sides of this central mass. His argument of the waste of material was met by the rejoinder that the walls must be strong enough to support the central block; and upon his replying that the central block was not supported by the sides, he was led to the top, and there made to see that this huge central mass was suspended like the clapper of a bell. On descending to the bottom, and lying on the ground, he could see, further, that there was an inch of space intervening between the soil and this mighty pendulum, which goes far towards securing the safety of the building during earthquakes. For centuries this centre of gravity has, by its swinging, been kept within the base; and it would assuredly be impossible to adduce stronger evidence of scientific forethought and calculation on the part of architects in dealing with a problem of extreme difficulty.''

In feudal times, the castle of the *daimyō* was wrought to a high degree of architectural excellence, with Feudal Castles. strong traces of Buddhistic influences. The most notable remaining specimen is that of

Nagoya, a city in central Japan, constructed in the year 1610 as a residence for Iyeyasu's son. It may be noted in the illustration that two golden dolphins surmount the five-storied donjon. One of these was sent to the Vienna Exposition of 1873, and on its way home went to the bottom of the ocean in consequence of a shipwreck. At length it was recovered, but with the greatest difficulty, and restored to its original situation, much to the satisfaction of the Japanese. These two ornaments measure eight and a half feet in height, being valued at $180,000. The dolphin, it may be remarked, is a Buddhist symbol.

Thus for many centuries the educational forces of Japan were entirely under Buddhist control. The monasteries were the first schools, and the monks were unfailing pedagogues. The state was utterly negligent of the intellectual culture of the people, and religion seized her golden opportunity. The temples throughout the whole country were converted into primary schools for all classes, and in the long period of the destructive civil wars, culture would have been absolutely lost had not the priests acted as its guardians. Not only so, but as with Europe in the dark ages, so also in Japan the monks became

THE GREAT CASTLE AT NAGOYA.

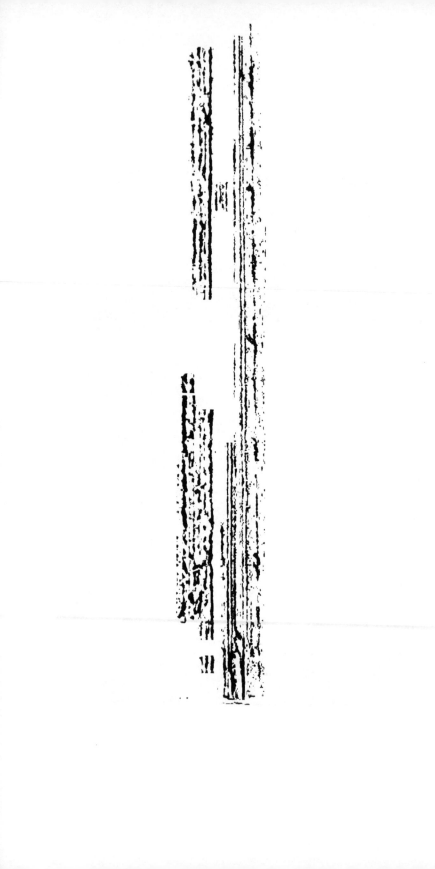

practical civilizers. "By the Buddhist priests many streams were spanned with bridges, paths and roads made, shade or fruit trees planted, ponds and ditches for purposes of irrigation dug, aqueducts built, unwholesome localities drained, and mountain passes discovered or explored." Little wonder that, as Mr. Lewis tells us, "before the end of the sixteenth century Buddhism had indelibly stamped itself on the language as well as the literature of Japan. The phraseology of the Japanese people was influenced by the Sûtras somewhat as our language has been influenced by the Bible."

With the coming of the seventeenth century, and the advent of the Tokugawa Shōgunate, Buddha began to be dis- Confucian placed by Confucius as the intel- Education. lectual leader of Japan. Buddhism retained its external dominion, but with characteristic plasticity accommodated itself to the Confucianist revival led by Iyeyasu, and began to teach the "Four Books" instead of the Sûtras. This remained the substance of education throughout the Tokugawa rule; and we see in the Confucian revival another evidence of Iyeyasu's statecraft. For Confucianism has been tersely described—not as

a religion, which it most certainly is not—
but as "a common ethico-political bond enabling millions of human beings to be governed from one centre." This fell in perfectly with the plans of Iyeyasu, and there
is no telling how much of the success of the
Tokugawa Shōgunate is due to the popular
instillation of Confucianist ideas. The edi-
tor and translator of the English edition of
the "Analects" has told us that "Confucius
was no transcendentalist; he never troubled
himself over such matters as first causes,
scarcely ever dealt with anything in the
abstract, knew nothing about science, and
not as much as one of our young school-
boys about the physical universe." Yet
his system was most arrogantly rigid, as
he laid down his rules for the race. He
has been called the Aristotle of Asia, whose
iron mould has produced in China for the
last two thousand years inflexible uniformity
of thought-processes, and prohibited origi-
nality.

The moral effects of Confucianism do not
speak any better for his system. While the
supreme doctrine of *chūkō* (fidelity to a
master and obedience to parents) has had
much to do with the perfection of Japanese

loyalty, as manifested in the national sentiment of Bushidō, the people seem to have achieved their other virtues rather in spite of Confucius than because of him. To his distinctly sceptical character may be traced the present sceptical attitude of the Japanese people; while, in view of his degrading doctrine of woman, it is remarkable that they should treat her with any consideration at all. A French scholar does no injustice whatever when he brings the scathing indictment—"Egoism, trickery, oppression of women and children, the prostitution of young girls, divorce laws for the benefit of men alone,—all these and many other facts are legitimate deductions from the Confucianist morality."

For two hundred and fifty years, the Buddhist priests being his school-masters, Confucius was the iron-handed mentor of Japan. Consequently, Western education had to take up its fight "against a flat, rectangular world, against a stationary plain with a gyrating sun, against alchemy, geomancy, astrology, and mental bondage," —to say nothing of moral obliquity.

The Result.

BOOK III

MODERN SCHOOL-DAYS

MODERN SCHOOL-DAYS
PART FIRST

THAT is the term above all others that describes the experience of modern Japan. The long period of Chinese culture was a season of inner development, wherein this race was gradually maturing towards the ability to receive an education that should be fitted to their strangely un-Oriental genius. For the East is by nature conservative, and Japan is by nature progressive. The East idolizes institutions, but Japan is intensely individual. Let him explain it who can, but the fact is that Japan is out of place in the Orient, being correctly described by the commonplace paradoxical phrase which calls her the yankeedom of Asia. Some serious scholars have contended that her people are indeed kinsmen to the aboriginal Americans, and that they found their way over the Pacific by means of the Arctic chain of islands. Certainly, the Japanese are temperamentally at variance with their neighbors, the Chinese and the Koreans, and with all of the other living races of Asia. They have even individualized their environment. Borrowing the civilization of China, they japanned it into a product of their own. Welcoming the poetry of Buddhism, they have defied its nihilism with scorn. Petulant of the interference of aliens, they had the original audacity to lock themselves up in their island and grow out their own character apart. Then when, in the middle of the nineteenth century, they suddenly came into their own, they threw off the shackles of Asia at a bound, and leaped straight into the freedom of the West. Their destiny had arrived, and they knew it. They have now had fifty years of Occidental schooldays, and they are lusty with the cry,—

> " Better fifty years of Europe
> Than a cycle of Cathay."

What shall their manhood be?

We have already traced the general preparation of the Japanese for the apt reception Special of Western civilization, and have Preparation. found it to consist in the harmonious development of five great qualities of character. But a special preparation was also taking place during the long reign of the Tokugawa Shōgunate, without which the

Perry expedition could never have been successful. This especial preparation was of a twofold character, being both intellectual and also political; these two streams of preparatory influence finally converging precisely in the nick of time to afford fair haven for the ships from over the sea.

By the irony of fate, it was Iyeyasu himself who first unbound the streams of intellectual influence that finally swept his successors off their feet. For, as we *Intellectual.* have already noted, the peaceful years of his later life were assiduously devoted to the revival of classical studies, and especially of the writings of Confucius, whose theories of government are so favorable to a centralized system like the Shōgunate. But there is a cardinal point in the Confucianist doctrine which the shrewd Shōgun must have overlooked; namely, that there can be but a *single* ruler of the people. This ruler, in the Confucian view, is the Emperor; and China nor any other country save Japan has ever known such a strange bicephalous arrangement as the Shōgunate. In theory, of course, the Iyeyasu system was correct: it has been shown many times throughout these pages that the Emperor was always theoretically supreme. But as the classical revival brought about by Iyeyasu gained ever greater impetus during the prolonged period of thoughtful leisure provided under Tokugawa rule, the scholars of Japan perceived more and more clearly that the classic doctrines which Iyeyasu had first taught them to revere are at heart opposed to the political system that had been perfected by his hands. Nor is this all. The history of education uniformly proves that, as a revival of learning proceeds, the ground of study invariably shifts from foreign to domestic fields. Just as, in Europe, the unfettering of the ancient languages led to the speedy development of European letters,—just as, in England, the invasion of the Norman culture was followed by a literary culture of our own; so in Japan the study of Confucius soon awakened an interest in the study of Japanese. The scholars delved into the forgotten depths of the early chronicles and discovered the modern origin of the Shōgunate. They perceived that the original government of their country was a pure imperialism such as the great Chinese sage laid down as the basis of all rule. They learned that the native religion of Japan was not Buddhism, but the ancient Shintō, which was at one with the doctrines of Confucius concerning the absolute power of the throne, and knew nothing of the upstart Shōgunate. As the Tokugawa family fell into the lassitude and luxury that had undermined the strength of the great clans before their day, the samurai scholars chafed more and more against this patent and unworthy usurpation; and when at length the opportunity came to hand, it was chiefly by the force of education that the Shōgunate was forever overthrown. "Knowledge is power." In this case it was doubly powerful, because it begot an intelligent patriotism in the most brave and loyal people of Asia, with whom devotion to their Emperor and to his rights became the rallying-cry that set him on a real throne. It is doubtful whether any other nation owes so much to the revolutionizing power of education. It was an educational revolution, under the leadership of Shōtoku Taishi, that moulded the history of Japan for thirteen centuries. The present era, which will be linked in native history forever with the name of the reigning Emperor Mutsuhito, is the most remarkable instance of an educational revolution that the world has ever seen, chiefly on account of its startling swiftness.

But it was really made possible by a gradual revolution on a smaller scale, proceeding under the intellectual leadership of the princes of Mito.

The second prince of Mito, Mitsukuni (A.D. 1622–1700), inherited the literary taste of his

The Mito Movement. illustrious grandfather, the founder of the Tokugawa Shōgunate. His natural talents were encouraged by circumstances that must by no means be overlooked if we would understand the modern history of Japanese educational development. It was in the province of Mito that those learned Chinese refugees found shelter who fled their native country on the overthrow of the Ming dynasty in the year 1644. Dr. Griffis likens the downfall of Pekin, in its influence on Japanese thought, to the downfall of Constantinople in relation to European development. The second prince of Mito had the best of opportunities for carrying forward those classical pursuits so dear to the heart of his grandfather. And he was soon stimulated thereby to the study of Japanese literature, which became the passion of his life. Gathering around him a company of kindred spirits, he began the compilation of the *Dai Nihon Shi*, a great "history of

Japan" in a hundred volumes, which his co-laborers brought to completion fifteen years after his death. Next to the two great products of early literature, the *Kojiki* and the *Nihongi*,* this huge work ranks as the most important history of Japan, which wrought such influence upon its readers as to lead that profound student of Japanese affairs, Sir Ernest Satow, to pronounce Mitsukuni "the real author of the movement which culminated in the revolution of 1868." For his history gained greater vogue as the years went by, being diligently studied in manuscript, until in 1851 the demand had become so general that it made its appearance in print, and became the mental food of the whole nation.

The second great literary offspring of the Mito movement had meanwhile made its appearance in 1827, from the pen of the eminent scholar Rai Sanyo. This was known as the *Nihon Gwaishi*, or "External History of Japan." The unconcealed aim of this immense undertaking, which occupied its author's time for twenty years continuously, was "to show that the Mikado is the only

---

* See page 60.

true ruler, in whom is the fountain of power, and to whom the allegiance of every Japanese is due; and that even the Tokugawas were not free from the guilt of usurpation." Professor Chamberlain speaks of its "fanatically imperialist sentiments, which contributed in no small measure to bring about the fall of the Shōgunate." He adds that the work is intolerably dry, so that the fact of a book like this having fired a whole nation with enthusiasm will ever remain one of the curiosities of literature. A prince of Mito in the year 1840 became so fervid for the restoration of the old true order of things that he actually resolved to exercise the samurai prerogative of allying the sword with the pen against the usurpation of the Shōgun. Hating Buddhism as an imported upstart religion and being zealous for the restoration of Shintō, he seized certain of the monasteries and melted their bells into cannon. But the Mito family handled the pen rather better than they wielded the sword, and this literary insurrection was suppressed; while it was left to the clans of the South to come to the aid of their literary northern brethren with secret preparations for war. Thus the unique twofold power of the samurai was made perfect by the union of southern swords with northern pens in common cause against a common foe.*

The southern antagonism against Toku-gawa rule doubtless had its remote beginnings in the early Chris-tian conquest of certain southern provinces, whose princes had become con-

Political Preparation for Reform.

---

* Japanese literature in general felt the impulse of the Mito movement. Clay MacCauley, in his essay on Japanese literature, tells us that what had been begun in the "Weeds of Idleness"—the amalgamation of a Chinese vocabulary with purely Japanese forms of speech—was well carried forward by the Mito school of historians towards the opening of the eighteenth century, and as this century advanced, was perfected by the accomplished critics, novelists, and dramatists of the times. To such critics as *Keichū* (1640–1701), *Mabu-chi* (1700–1769), *Motowori* (1730–1800), and *Hirata* (1776–1843), Japanese literature is indebted for elabo-rate critical commentaries on the "Kojiki," the "Man-yōshū," and the ancient Shintō ritual; and from them the writers of later days received models in composition and style. Chamberlain says of Motowori, indeed, that as a stylist he stands alone among Japanese writers, being altogether the "greatest scholar and writer of modern Japan." *Bakin* (1767–1840) and *Ikku* (1763–1831) are the greatest of Japanese novelists, the latter being sometimes compared with Rabelais; while the two most famous dramatists of the Tokugawa period were *Takeda* (1690–1756) and *Chikamitsu* (1652–1724), "the Japanese Shakespeare."

verts to the faith and thereby the outlaws
of Iyeyasu and Iyemitsu, bequeathing to their
posterity a hatred of the Tokugawa rule
which might smoulder but could never go out.
The Shimabara massacre left an awful scar
on the memories of the people of Kyūshū.
Not only so, but they could not forget that
southern demigod, Hideyoshi, whose most
powerful generals had been southern men,
equal with Iyeyasu in the Taikō's wars, only
to see the Shōgunate usurped and themselves
dishonored by the murderer of Hideyoshi's
son and mother. This spirit of slumbering
antagonism to the Tokugawa rule never once
died out in the breasts of the Satsuma and
Chōshū clans, in the extreme south-western
provinces of Kyūshū and Hondo respectively.
They cherished the lessons they had learned
from the deported foreigners in the bloody
science of war. The prince of Satsuma sys-
tematically encouraged the acquirement of all
foreign learning that might give superiority
against the Shōgun. He cared not for the foreigners themselves, and still less for the religion of his ancestors; but he hated the Tokugawa rule. By hook or crook he contrived to
get hints and clues of science from the hermit
Dutch colony at Nagasaki. He actually suc-

ceeded in the erection of foundries for the manufacture of cannon and other western weapons. He encouraged the study of western languages in order to learn western secrets, and even succeeded in sending a score of disciples abroad, eluding the vigilance of the Shōgunate, that they might return and revolutionize Japan. These southern activities account for the fact that, in spite of Japan's long seclusion, Commodore Perry found men who were "not only well-bred, but not ill-educated." In the official narrative of his expedition we are told that "when a terrestrial globe was placed before them, and their attention was called to the delineation on it of the United States, they immediately placed their fingers on Washington and New York, as if perfectly familiar with the fact that one was the capital and the other the commercial metropolis of our country. . . . They also inquired whether the canal across the isthmus was as yet finished." * Can it be that this nimble-witted race took for granted the completion of a work so essential, whereas we have barely begun it fifty years after their question was asked? This at least seems as

---

* "Narrative," etc., New York, 1857, page 248.

13

reasonable a view as the labored comment of the learned narrator. He tells us further that "they seemed to acquire rapidly some insight into the nature of steam and the mode with which it was applied to put into action the great engine and move by its power the wheels of the steamers. Their questions were of the most intelligent character."

This brings us at length to the expedition under Commodore Perry, one of the most ro- The Perry mantic and dramatic events in mod- Expedition. ern history.

There had been various attempts to unlock the doors of Japan after Iyemitsu closed them in 1624. Within two hundred years Great Britain made nine such unsuccessful efforts, the Dutch two, and the Russians three. America's first attempt occurred in the year 1837, to be repeated in 1846 and 1849, without success. Finally, in 1852, the government authorized and equipped the expedition which owed its success chiefly to the ability of the mariner-statesman who both suggested and commanded it, Commodore Matthew Calbraith Perry.

The objects that America had in view were of the most practical and prosaic character. They are naïvely stated in the letter

addressed by President Fillmore to his ''great
and good friend,'' the Emperor of Japan,
but presented by mistake to the
Shōgun. ''Our great State of America's Aims.
California,'' wrote the President, ''produces
about sixty millions of dollars in gold every
year, besides silver, quicksilver, precious
stones, and many other valuable articles. I
am desirous that our two countries should
trade with each other.'' Again: ''I have
directed Commodore Perry to mention another thing to your imperial majesty. Many
of our ships pass every year from California
to China; and great numbers of our people
pursue the whale fishery near the shores of
Japan. It sometimes happens, in stormy
weather, that one of our ships is wrecked on
your imperial majesty's shores. In all such
cases we ask, and expect, that our unfortunate people should be treated with kindness,
and that their property should be protected
till we can send a vessel and bring them
away.'' Thus it would appear, as a Japanese writer suggests, that Michelet was not so
very far wrong when he cried, ''Who opened
to men the great distant navigation? Who
revealed the ocean and marked out its zones
and its liquid highways? Who discovered the

secrets of the globe? The whale and the whales!" American capital was at this time invested in the whaling fisheries near the coasts of Japan to the extent of about seventeen million dollars. But there was a third reason for the Perry expedition. "Commodore Perry is also directed by me to represent to your imperial majesty that we understand that there is a great abundance of coal and provisions in the Empire of Japan," continues the President. "Our steamships, in crossing the great ocean, burn a great deal of coal, and it is not convenient to bring it all the way from America. We wish that our steamships and other vessels should be allowed to stop in Japan and supply themselves with coal, provisions, and water. We are very desirous of this."

It would therefore appear that three simple commercial considerations prompted the Perry expedition,—better coaling facilities; better whaling facilities; and the extension of California commerce consequent upon the discovery of gold in 1848.

As one reads the interesting narrative of this expedition, admiration deepens into wonder over the manner in which its commander conducted the pro-

Perry's Ability.

longed and difficult negotiations,—evincing the powers of a finished but firm diplomatist, with long years of experience in the courts of the subtle East, whereas his honors hitherto had all been won in rough battle, either with the seas or with his country's enemies. In one of his letters to the government he shows the rarest understanding of Oriental character when he says that in dealing with people of forms "it is necessary either to set all ceremony aside, or to out-Herod Herod in assumed personal consequence and ostentation."

Commodore Perry, in dealing with the most ceremonial people on earth, proved himself able to "hoist them with their own petard." Upon anchoring in *His success.* the Bay of Yedo on July 8, 1853, he refused at once to give audience to any official who was not his equal in rank and duly accredited to deal with him. When excited officials came and besought him to go to the open port of Nagasaki, he firmly refused, and demanded an embassy from the Emperor. When, finally, the Shōgun (whom he always mistook for the Emperor) sent him this princely embassy and received him with all pomp and ceremony, one knows not whether to be chiefly amused or amazed by the manner in which the letter of our democratic president was delivered. The narrative, after describing the impressive landing of the marines and their pompous procession to the hall of audience, especially erected for this meeting, informs us that "two boys, dressed for the ceremony, preceded the Commodore bearing in an envelope of scarlet cloth the boxes which contained his credentials and the President's letter. These documents, of folio size, were beautifully written on vellum, and not folded, but bound in blue silk velvet. Each seal, attached by cords of interwoven gold and silk with pendant gold tassels, was encased in a circular box six inches in diameter and three in depth, wrought of pure gold. Each of the documents, together with its seal, was placed in a box of rosewood about a foot long, with lock, hinges, and mountings, all of gold. On either side of the Commodore marched a tall, well-formed negro, who, armed to the teeth, acted as his personal guard. These blacks, selected for the occasion, were two of the best-looking fellows of their color that the squadron could furnish. All this, of course, was but for effect."

It produced a tremendous effect, but not so much as the Commodore's firmness, backed by his terrible engines of war. The islanders had been greatly excited *Perry's Wisdom.* by the appearance of his four "black ships of evil mien," freighted with great open-mouthed guns. A native writer tells us that "the popular commotion in Yedo at the news of 'a foreign invasion' was beyond description. The whole city was in an uproar. In all directions were seen mothers flying with children in their arms, and men with mothers on their backs. Rumors of an immediate action, exaggerated each time they were communicated from mouth to mouth, added horror to the horror-stricken." In a day or two, however, as it was made clear that the invaders were peaceful, terror changed to curiosity, and the officials, making a virtue of necessity, consented, as we have seen, to transmit the President's letter to the Shōgun in Yedo, whom they permitted Commodore Perry always to regard as the Emperor. Having secured this important concession, the Commodore with remarkable sagacity steamed away to China with the promise to return for an answer during the following spring. His first visit lasted only eight days.

In this brief time, besides accomplishing the main object of his visit, he succeeded in establishing convivial relations with Japanese officials, whom he entertained on board his flagship; and even secured their consent to a significant interchange of presents. Moreover, before his departure he boldly sailed his squadron up the bay almost to the gates of the capital city, which lies some thirty miles north of his original anchorage. The intelligent Japanese perceived that their capital was entirely at the mercy of his great men-of-war, but that he abstained from the use of force. Having produced a tremendous effect upon the advisers and officials of the Shōgunate, the Commodore sailed away and gave them time to think it over. Besides, his presence was needed in China, and he also wished to come with still greater show of force when demanding a proper answer to his letter.

On the 13th day of February, 1854, Commodore Perry again anchored in the Bay of Perry's Second Visit. Yedo, being now in command of a fleet of eight stately vessels. We have no time to follow the negotiations in detail. Suffice it to say that the American sailor gave continual evidence of his remarkable skill in diplomacy; and that he finally secured, on the 31st of March, the execution of a formal treaty that secured for America all of the objects desired. After a sojourn of more than four months, including an important visit to Yezo on account of the whaling interests, the squadron took its departure, and Japan was opened to the world. England and Russia were quick to make treaties, and other nations speedily followed. In its effect upon the history of the world, the Perry expedition is probably the most important peaceful voyage undertaken since the expedition of Columbus. It is by no means unlikely that Columbus himself was seeking the land of Japan, whereof his adventurous countryman, Marco Polo, had brought the first tidings to Europe.* But Columbus, instead of finding the farthest country of the East, discovered the world of the West. Two and a half centuries later, it was the lot of the young Western nation to complete his unfulfilled endeavor and unbar the gateways of Asia. For the events of recent years are proving that Japan is the key to the Orient.

It is interesting to notice the character of

---

* See "Mikado's Empire," Griffis, page 247.

the presents exchanged between the East and the West on the occasion of the negotiation Exchange of Gifts. of the treaty. Among the principal objects presented by the "Emperor," as the Americans invariably called him, to the President of the United States, was a "censer of bronze (cow-shape), supporting silver flower and stand." The bovine design was very puzzling to the minds of the westerners, but we have already learned that in Japanese usage the cow is a symbol of education, from its association with the great Michizane, their high-priest of letters.* Other prominent articles were book-cases and writing-tables; so it would appear without doubt that the Shōgun expressed by this symbolism his understanding of education as the key-note to the progress of the West. Chief among the American presents, alas! were rifles and muskets, pistols and swords,—and the Japanese have learned the lesson right well. There were also numerous baskets of champagne, with plenty of whiskey and wine, which played an important part, as we are told, in establishing cordial and even convivial relations with the natives.

---

* See page 168.

On the other hand, there were books, telegraph equipments, and a pygmy locomotive outfit. With reference to this last, the narrator graphically informs us that "all the parts of the mechanism were perfect, and the car was a most tasteful specimen of workmanship, but so small that it could hardly carry a child of six years of age. The Japanese, however, were not to be cheated out of a ride, and, as they were unable to reduce themselves to the capacity of the inside of the carriage, they betook themselves to the roof. It was a spectacle not a little ludicrous to behold a dignified mandarin whirling around the circular road at the rate of twenty miles an hour, with his loose robes flying in the wind. As he clung with a desperate hold to the edge of the roof, grinning with intense interest, and his huddled-up body shook convulsively with a kind of laughing timidity, while the car spun rapidly around the circle, you might have supposed that the movement, somehow or other, was dependent rather upon the enormous exertions of the uneasy mandarin than upon the power of the little puffing locomotive, which was so easily performing its work." But there is more than a mere joke in this picture. It strikingly illustrates the intellectual alertness of the Japanese, who, albeit perhaps the most sensitive people on earth, are even willing to subject themselves to what one of their living educators calls "the greatest evil,"—namely, ridicule,—in order to acquire new knowledge. The moment they were convinced that the outside world had good things which they did not possess, they resolved to become possessors at any cost. Dr. Griffis believes that "the noblest trait in the character of a Japanese is his willingness to change for the better when he discovers his wrong or inferiority."

And yet the cold prosaic fact remains that the chief reason why the "barbarian" Ameri-

The Shōgun's Dilemma. cans were allowed to enter Japan was simply that the Shōgunate was too weak to keep them out. It is one thing to speak of Japanese character, and quite a different matter to treat of Japanese politics. It was with extreme reluctance that the Shōgun concluded his treaty with America, making a virtue of necessity, as already stated. And when he did yield to the importunities of Commodore Perry it was only to find himself entangled in a web of difficulties within the realm itself. Here it is necessary to recall the interior preparation for revolution that had been going forward for so many years under the literary leadership of the princes of Mito and the military direction of the Sat-Chō (Satsuma-Chōshū) clans. The patriotism of these forces was intense; they believed in ''Japan for the Japanese'' and in a restored Mikado. They were therefore united both in their hatred for the obtrusive Shōgunate and in their hatred for the intrusive foreigners. Had not the prince of Satsuma, in 1837, deliberately decoyed the American naval vessel ''Morrison'' into his harbors, and then fired on it? As for the prince of Mito, no sooner did he hear of the negotiations that were taking place on the occasion of Perry's first visit, than he presented the Shōgun with an urgent protest against them. It is significant that he plunges at once into the subject of religion. ''Notwithstanding the strict interdiction of Christianity,'' he declares, ''there are those guilty of the heinous crime of professing the doctrines of this evil sect. If now America be once admitted into our favor, the rise of this faith is a matter of certainty.'' He concludes his strenuous memorial with a ringing call to arms against the despised barbarians. ''Peace and prosperity of long duration have enervated the spirit, rusted the armor, and blunted the swords of our men. Dulled to ease, when shall they be aroused? Is not the present the most auspicious moment to quicken their sinews of war?" Almost all of the *daimyōs* shared the opinions of Mito, and opposed the opening of the country. But the Shōgunate had seen the "four black ships of evil mien," and knew that Perry could not be opposed. In a nervous panic they threw up a few harmless forts in the Bay of Yedo, indeed, during Perry's absence in China; but they had no heart in their task. During this same crucial period of suspense, the Shōgun Iyeyoshi died, and his son Iyesada awaited the return of the foreigner in the midst of a turmoiled government and in the face of a deadly opposition. Plainly, the Shōgunate was tottering to its fall.

Perry returned; Iyesada succumbed to the inevitable, and threw in his lot with the foreigners. As soon as the treaty was signed, the opposition flew into a fury. The *Jō-i* party was formed, with the Prince of Mito at its head; the name means, "expel the barbarians." The Sat-Chō party eagerly seized the opportunity for giving vent to their cherished hatred of the Tokugawas.

Opposition.

This hatred was wrought to a white heat when it was learned that the treaties had been signed at Yedo without consulting with Kyōto at all. The Emperor Kōmei had been ignored. The literary patriots took advantage of this fact to remind the thoughtless masses that they really had an emperor, and that he was by rights their only ruler. The Shōgunate, usurping the imperial prerogatives, had concluded a treaty of peace and commerce with the barbarians! Kōmei himself, a man of no little ability, declared that his rest was disturbed by the spectacle of "the fierce barbarian at our very door." For the first time in centuries the imperial voice was heard and heeded, and the country resounded with the cry, "Honor the Emperor, expel the barbarian!" After a peace of two and a half centuries, Japan made ready for war.

But so great was the confusion of this turbulent period that it can hardly be dignified with the name of war. Japan was experiencing the terrors of a prolonged political earthquake. As if to symbolize this fact, the troubles of the ill-starred Shōgunate were enlarged in 1855 when a literal and most terrific earthquake laid the

Turmoil.

capital city in ruins. Japan is visited with an average of an earthquake for every day in the year; but seldom has this country of cataclysms suffered more severely than by this fearful disaster, which destroyed fifteen thousand dwellings, and was followed by an awful conflagration. The ignorant not unnaturally attributed the ruin of Yedo to the wickedness of its rulers, and were the more eager to see them utterly overthrown.

We may follow the confusions of this revolutionary period, which culminated in 1868, only in the largest outline. The Shō-

Conflict.

gunate recovered somewhat of its influence upon the death of Iyesada, in 1858, when the government was seized by the regent Ii, who established himself in power by the ancient trick of setting an infant ruler on a nominal throne. As successor to the Shōgunate he selected a twelve-year-old boy named Iyemochi, whom he could easily control, while utterly ignoring the Mikado. This stroke of Ii's, in fact, was but the Hōjō usurpation on a smaller scale. He meted out instant and terrible punishment upon all who labored for the restoration of imperialism, and by sheer personal force cemented the crumbling power of Yedo into a temporary resistance against its foes. But the arrogance of his usurpation added flocks of new followers to the *Jō-i* party and their associates in the south, besides causing hordes of *rōnin* to take to the field pledged never to rest until the Emperor should be restored to his throne. Ii fell a victim to these "wave-men" by assassination, and his downfall was the signal for murderous attacks upon the foreigners and the destruction of the foreign legations. The real power of the Shōgunate now fell into the hands of a strong party who committed themselves wholly to the admission of Western influences, signalizing this fact in the year 1860 by sending an embassy of inquiry abroad. But in order to conciliate the sentiment at home, the nominal Shōgun, Iyemochi, was now persuaded by his advisers to renew the ancient custom of paying a visit of homage to the Emperor at Kyōto, in recognition of his theoretical supremacy. The effect of this journey was simply to demonstrate to the hitherto unmoved masses that the Shōgun was, after all, an inferior; and the virile Emperor, moreover, took advantage of this opportunity so to exert his influence upon the weak Shōgun, as to secure the appointment of a prime minister who was in collusion with the Sat-Chō clans. The first act of this premier was to abolish the ancient rule of Iyemitsu which required the *daimyōs* to make their residence at Yedo. "Like wild birds from an opened cage, they, with all their retainers, fled from the city in less than a week." "And so," says the native chronicler, "the prestige of the Tokugawa family, which had endured for three hundred years; which had been really more brilliant than Kamakura in the age of Yoritomo on a moonlight night when the stars are shining; which for more than two hundred and seventy years had forced the *daimyōs* to come breathlessly to take their turn of duty in Yedo, and which had, day and night, eighty thousand vassals at its beck and call, fell to ruin in the space of one morning."

The Shōgunate party, in a desperate endeavor to recover its lost prestige, now

Final Struggles of the Shōgunate.

wheeled about and attempted to close the country against foreigners. In this there was unity of action, for the Emperor also officially expelled all "barbarians" from Japan. The Sat-Chō clans, emboldened by the weakening of the Shōgun's government, fired from their forts on the ships of France, Holland, and the United States, gathered in Shimonoseki Straits (between Hondo and Kyūshū) in July, 1863, and shortly afterwards attacked a steamer belonging to the Shōgunate. The three powers took redress, assisted by Great Britain, in the following year; bombarding Shimonoseki, and thus bringing the fierce Sat-Chō clansmen a salutary lesson in barbarian strength. Unfortunate Yedo was also made to suffer, the combined powers demanding of the Shōgunate, as the only responsible government, an indemnity of three million dollars for the assault of the Chōshū men. Iyemochi thereupon attempted to punish the southern clansmen for the indignity they had brought upon Japan, being emboldened to take these measures by a success that his troops had won against the southerners at Kyōto. But the time had now come for a decisive test of strength, and the Chōshū warriors proved the long preparations they had been making for this struggle with the hated Shōgunate. "The Chōshū clansmen, united and alert, were lightly dressed, armed with English and American rifles, drilled in European tactics, and abundantly provided with

The Shimonoseki Affair.

artillery, which they fired rapidly and with precision. They had cast away armor, sword, and spear. Chōshū had long been the seat of Dutch learning, and translations of Dutch military works were numerously made and used there. Their disciplined battalions were recruited from the common people, not from the samurai alone, were well paid, and full of enthusiasm. The Shōgunate had but a motley, half-hearted army, many of whom, when the order was given to march, straightway fell ill, having no stomach for the fight.'' The campaign ended in the utter defeat of the Shōgunate, whose exhausted leader, Iyemochi, died at Ōsaka in 1866.

This brings the last of the Shōguns upon the scene. The dramatic circumstances of his career invest this man, Hitotsubashi, with such a glamour of romance that it is very difficult to determine his real character. By some writers he is criticised as a vacillating weakling, while others praise him as the equal in unselfishness of George Washington—who, by the way, is one of the national heroes of young Japan. We will simply let the complex story speak for itself.

The Last of the Shōguns.

The waxing power of the Emperor appears

in the fact that this Shōgun was appointed
directly by the court. Not only so, but he was
a son of the Prince of Mito, being thus of the
Tokugawa clan, but brought up under strong
imperialistic influences. So strong had been
his influence with the Emperor that he had
succeeded, as Iyemochi's guardian, in securing the imperial consent to the foreign treaties (1865). Thus the chief stigma had been
removed from the Shōgunate in connection
with the foreigners. Yet it is said that Hitotsu-bashi was not really friendly to the foreigners, and endeavored afterwards to bring
about their exclusion. However, by a strange
set of circumstances, this loyalist Shōgun
shortly found himself in the position of
antagonizing the court. This was brought
about by a master-stroke on the part of the
Sat-Chō men, who took advantage of the
death of the Emperor Kōmei early in the
year 1867 to effect a *coup d'état*. Their
wisest counsellors secured complete control of the young Emperor, Mutsuhito,
"the man of meekness," at that time only
fifteen years old; while their troops assumed the name of "the loyal army" and
surrounded the palace at Kyōto. Immediately an edict went forth dissolving the

Shōgunate, and proclaiming Mutsuhito sole ruler of the empire. Hitotsu-bashi realized that this was wholly the work of the traditional enemies of his house, and he also perceived that the Shōgunate was doomed, by an immemorial rule, so long as the imperial person was in the possession of the enemy. In this extremity he led his forces in an assault against "the loyal army," but was repulsed from the neighborhood of Kyōto with heavy loss. He could easily have recruited his forces, and prolonged the struggle indefinitely. But the principle of loyalty was so strong in him that he refused to appear in the attitude of rebellion, albeit by the trick of his enemies, and he therefore resolved to resign. There can be no doubt that he was also more than half a convert to the literary doctrines of his father's house, for in a final letter to his vassals we read the words: "It appears to me that the laws cannot be maintained in face of the daily extension of our foreign relations, unless the government be conducted by one head, and I therefore propose to surrender the whole governing power into the hands of the imperial court. This is the best I can do for the interests of the empire." His resignation was presented on the 19th of November, 1867, and a system which had endured for nearly seven centuries was The Shōgun brought forever to an end; it Resigns. being simply inconceivable that circumstances will ever again be such as to admit the formation of that singular institution of government which evolved in Yoritomo's time into the Shōgunate. Hitotsu-bashi was the last of his line. He retired to the ancient home of Iyeyasu, in Shizuoka, and there sought a quiet retreat for his last declining days. In a great storehouse on his estate the rust and the mildew have wrought havoc with the heaps of costly gifts "presented by the government of the United States to the Emperor of Japan." The Emperor never saw them. They were very costly gifts, for they cost the Shōguns their rule.*

No sooner had the Sat-Chō cabinet which surrounded the Emperor accomplished the

---

* "It is on record that the last of the Shōguns—oh, infinite pathos!—rides an American model in these his last feeble days—days whose sole light is, so to speak, a spirit-lamp of glorious memories—the memories of an inheritor of such dominion as Cæsar wielded, the sadly glorious memories of an inheritor who has lost his inheritance."—W. P. WATSON, " Japan," 1904.

overthrow of the Shōgunate, than they achieved the most rapid reversion of policy Sudden whereof history bears any record. Change. That is to say, they at once faced about and marched in the direction of progress. They gave themselves and the new imperial régime to a whole-souled "westernization" of which the half-hearted Shōgunate had never faintly dreamed. They went so far at the very beginning as to advance the startling proposition that the inviolate practice of untold ages should be broken, and that the Emperor ought to come out from his mysterious seclusion and mingle with his people after the fashion of the monarchs of the West. As if this were not enough to take the breath away, it was further proposed that the sacred capital at Kyōto should be abandoned, although it had been the imperial residence since 794 A.D., and the Emperor remove to Yedo, renamed "Tōkyō," "the eastern capital," thus signalizing the downfall of the Shōgunate and the actual sovereignty of the quondam pūppet-emperor. These propositions were made by Ōkubo of Satsuma in the red-letter "year of restoration," 1868, as follows: "Since the Middle Ages, our Emperor has lived behind a screen, and has never trodden the earth. Nothing of what went on outside his screen ever penetrated his sacred ear; the imperial residence was profoundly secluded, Ōkubo's Proposal. and, naturally, unlike the outer world. Not more than a few court nobles were allowed to approach the throne, a practice most opposed to the principles of heaven. Although it is the first duty of man to respect his superior, if he reveres that superior too highly he neglects his duty, while a breach is created between the sovereign and his subjects, who are unable to convey their wants to him. This vicious practice has been common in all ages. But now let pompous etiquette be done away, and simplicity become our first object. Kyōto is in an out-of-the-way position, and is unfit to be the seat of government. Let His Majesty take up his abode temporarily at Ōsaka, removing his capital thither, and thus cure one of the hundred abuses which we inherit from past ages.'' Circumstances considered, this is one of the boldest utterances ever made by mortal man. The nation was dumfounded by the proposed innovations, while the *daimyōs* stood aghast at the sudden and extreme radicalism of the supposed conservatives of the south. Enmities were en-

gendered in the Satsuma clan which culminated several years later in "the Satsuma
rebellion," and in the assassination of
Ōkubo. But the startling changes were made,
simply because Ōkubo and his powerful associates were in control of the government.
More was granted than had been asked, because it was decided not to make a merely
temporary capital at Ōsaka, but to remove
The "Meiji" permanently to "the eastern cap-
Period.   ital" at once. A new era was
chosen for Japanese history, beginning with
the year 1868, and it received the significant
name of the *Meiji* period, which means
"progress." In February of that year the
young Emperor still further astonished the
conservative element by inviting the foreign
representatives in Japan to an imperial audience, the significance of which can hardly
now be conceived. "Never before in the history of the empire had its divine head deigned
to admit to his presence the despised foreigner, or to put himself on an equality with
the sovereign of the foreigner." The
event created the most profound excitement. The escort of the British minister was attacked on its way to the palace, and compelled to retire. But the court

was inexorably committed to progress, and a successful audience was conducted on the following day. Not only so, but the Emperor now issued an edict protecting the foreigners, and decreeing capital punishment of the most disgraceful character against any who might molest them. The year 1868 was the year of imperial restoration, and the beginning of the "Progress Period" of new Japan. It is the most important mile-stone in Japanese history for thirteen centuries, or since the deliberate reception of Chinese culture in the reign of the Empress Suiko.*

Notable events succeeded with such tremendous rapidity that it is difficult to present them in their due proportion. But it would be impossible to exaggerate the importance of a memorial which appeared in the "Official Gazette" of March 5, 1869. It was signed by the most powerful *daimyōs* of the South, was addressed to the Emperor, and amounted in fact to the voluntary abolition of feudalism. The Shōgun had resigned his Shōgunate, the barons now resign their fiefs. The patriotic eloquence of these feudal lords reached its acme in the

Resignation of the Daimyōs.

* See page 56.

words: "The place where we live is the Emperor's land and the food that we eat is grown by the Emperor's men. How can we claim it as our own? We now reverently offer up the list of our possessions and followers, with the prayer that the Emperor will take good measures for rewarding those to whom reward is due and for fining those to whom punishment is due. Let the imperial orders be issued for altering and remodelling the territories of the various clans. Let the civil and penal codes, the military laws down to the rules for uniform and the construction of engines of war, all proceed from the Emperor. Let all the affairs of the Empire, both great and small, be referred to him."

If the Sat-Chō clans had seen their long-cherished desire fulfilled in the resignation of the Tokugawa Shōgun, then the cup of the house of Mito must have been filled to overflowing by this absolute restoration of imperialism effected by the resignation of the *daimyōs*. Yet this also was the work of the

Itō.

Southerners. A young Chōshū samurai named Itō had been among those that had eluded the Shōgun's vigilance in the hermit days, eventually succeeding in working his way before the mast of a foreign vessel, all the way to far-off London. His eyes were opened by what he saw there, and "he returned to put his head to extraordinary uses." It is now known that Itō was the real author of this celebrated document,— although it was engineered to success by Kido, another southern clansman, sometimes known as "the brain of the Restoration." It may as well be said at this point that the southern clansmen retain entire control of the government to this day, in spite of a constitution that grants equality of rights to all. They do so, however, by virtue of their intellectual ability and dominant force of character, so that, while the constitution suffers, the state not only survives but finds its chief source of strength in these statesmen. Of Itō we shall learn more hereafter. It is significant of his illustrious career that his first political achievement should be of such tremendous importance as the voluntary abolition of feudalism.

But the Emperor was not to be outdone. He accepted the surrender of feudalism, but declined to rule in the spirit of absolutism. On April 17, 1869, the youthful Mutsuhito appeared before his court and an assembly of powerful *daimyōs* to take

The Charter Oath.

his famous "charter oath," in substance as follows: (1) A deliberative assembly shall be formed, and all measures decided by public opinion; (2) the principles of social and political science shall be diligently studied by all classes; (3) equal rights shall be accorded to all who strive for a worthy purpose; (4) all the absurd usages of former times shall be disregarded, and the impartiality and justice displayed in the operations of nature adopted as the basis of action; (5) wisdom and ability shall be sought in all sections of the globe for the purpose of firmly establishing the foundations of empire. This oath is the basis of the present government, and its promises have been performed with surprising thoroughness. Within the year a tentative parliament was held, and the Emperor

A New Capital.
also took up his residence in the Tokugawa palace at Tōkyō, where he still resides. Japan was fairly launched upon that career of progress that has made her the modern marvel of the world.

We must break the chain of events at this point to inquire briefly into the causes of that sudden and startling change on the part of the imperial advisers which transformed them in a trice from the bitterest enemies of the West into Occidentalists of the most pronounced type, who straightway thrust Japan loose from her rusty mediæval moorings full into the great rushing current of world politics.

The change cannot be understood unless we keep clearly in mind two fundamental Japanese characteristics, namely, their intense patriotism and their remarkable intellectual flexibility. Everything that Japan does is to be accounted for by her undying patriotism. In no country is there greater attachment to the native land. Feuds and jealousies may spring up at home, but these gain their chief fierceness from the very fact that each warring faction is tenaciously devoted to some pet policy which it conceives as best adapted to advance the interests of the country. Thus, Hitotsu-bashi was unquestionably a patriot, but so were the Sat-Chō men. These regarded the Shōgunate as a usurpation, and deemed the restoration of the Emperor to be imperative for the welfare of the land. But during the course of the restoration, their agile intellects received salutary lessons from the West. Chōshū learned at Shimonoseki, as Satsuma had learned at Kagōshima,* that Japan in her seclusion had by no means kept pace with "barbarian" nations in the arts of war, even as Itō declared. Moreover, the handful of young men who visited Europe in those early days returned, as they themselves tell us, "with their faces flushed with enthusiastic sympathy with the modern civilization of Christendom." So it was that in the very course of their warfare with the Shōgunate, a warfare directly precipitated by the Western question, these keen and pliable intellects were doubtless convinced that the welfare of their country could be best advanced by the adoption of Occidental civilization. It was the Shōgunate that they fought. And when this had been overthrown, the same patriotic impulse that had impelled the victors, now enlightened by the dazzling glow of the western sun, caused them to adopt the very policy that had led to the outbreak of their war.

But throughout the years that immediately

---

* A British squadron bombarded and almost annihilated the Satsuma capital in 1863 in reprisal for the murder of a British subject by exasperated Satsuma retainers the year before.

preceded the great restoration of 1868, southern clansmen had had unusual opportunities for the reception of Western enlightenment. Not only the lurid light of war, but the softer luminary of peace and good-will shone upon them from the neighboring western shores. One cannot say too much for the influence, in those early days, of the American missionary-teachers who, in their eagerness to bring the light, landed in the erstwhile "Christian" city of Nagasaki before the treaties fairly accorded them that right. The first to arrive was the Rev. John Liggins, an Englishman with an American training, who had been engaged in missionary work in China.* He landed on the 2d of May, 1859, and was joined a month later by a colleague from China, the Rev. C. M. Williams, who devoted his life to the awakening empire. Both of these gentlemen represented the Protestant Episcopal Church. They were followed in October of the same year by Dr. J. C. Hepburn, a medical missionary of

The First Protestant Missionaries.

---

* This distinguished man is still living. The author was honored by a letter from his pen in the summer of 1904.

the Presbyterian Church, while the Dutch Reformed Church immediately added the services of Dr. D. B. Simmons and the Rev. S. R. Brown. But this notable missionary year, 1859, was chiefly signalized by the arrival in November of Verbeck,—that great "man without a country," born in Holland, schooled in America, married until his death in 1898 to the welfare of the new Japan,—who, more than any and all others, became schoolmaster to the Emperor's advisers, and consequently an untold influence in the creation of the Japan of to-day.

There is room for but the briefest sketch of this powerful career in connection with the opening years of the new Japan.[*]

Verbeck.

Brief as it is, it must not be overlooked by those who would weigh the causes that made the Japanese Revolution. As with all of the earliest missionaries except Dr. Hepburn, Verbeck made his headquarters at Nagasaki. His associates and the hosts that came after them have done a noble work for Christianity in Japan; but, owing to his peculiar equipment and opportunities, Verbeck from the very beginning gained a grip

---

[*] See the fuller sketch in "Japan To-Day."

on the government itself that makes his story absolutely unique. Being in Nagasaki, he was near the great dominant *daimyōs*, and being the man that he was, he succeeded in reaching them.   This was by virtue of a singularly engaging personality, coupled with a culture that was at once versatile and thorough.   He was versed in the European languages, and had also had training in science. His intellect was strongly creative, and, best of all, he had sense.   Attracting the attention of the young samurai who thronged Nagasaki in quest of Dutch learning, his little home soon became an embryo Japanese university. At his feet sat scores of the men who, largely by reason of his training, were destined to direct the future course of empire. His fame spreading, by the year 1867 four of the foremost princes were clamoring for him to come to their provinces and direct that foreign progress which they were now so eager to advance among their people. It was his own fair example of what a westerner may be that confirmed them in this eagerness; and none can guess what weighty share his skilful hand possessed in those plastic days towards the moulding of the brand-new government. We know certainly that when the capital was

established at Tōkyō, Verbeck was immediately sent for; and so, after a decade of
unmeasured usefulness in the southern sea-
port, he became the director of the forming
university and man-of-all-work to the government. Shortly he was the teacher of a
thousand eager learners, a second Abélard;
besides being busied with the translation of
such great works as the Napoleonic Code,
Blackstone's Commentaries, Humboldt's Cos-
mos, Bluntschli's and Wheaton's and Perry's
treatises on political economy and international law,—massive foundations for the
building of a mighty nation. One who visited
him in 1871 gives this graphic inner glimpse
of the great missionary's workshop: "I saw
a prime minister of the empire, heads of departments, and officers of various ranks,
whose personal and official importance I
sometimes did and sometimes did not realize, coming to find out from Mr. Verbeck matters of knowledge or to discuss
with him points and courses of action.
To-day it might be a plan of national education; to-morrow, the engagement of foreigners to important positions; or the despatch
of an envoy to Europe; the choice of the language best suitable for medical science; or

how to act in matters of neutrality between France and Germany, whose war-vessels were in Japanese waters; or to learn the truth about what some foreign diplomatist had asserted; or concerning the persecutions of Christians; or some serious measure of home policy.''

Note that phrase, ''concerning the persecutions of Christians.'' It must not be imagined that, because Verbeck was accorded such very high honors, his missionary propaganda was encouraged. Japan was endeavoring to receive the Western civilization while rejecting the westerners' religion. No sooner had the new government been established than it republished the old interdicts against Christianity, and followed these up with new. For, now that the country was opened to foreigners again, it was discovered that there were hundreds who still held the old tradition handed down to them by their fathers, and that they mistook the removal of the interdict against foreigners as being also a removal of the embargo against the foreigners' religion. A most interesting incident occurred in 1865 in Nagasaki, where incoming Roman Catholic missionaries had

Renewed Persecutions.

Prolonged Fidelity of Christians.

made bold to erect a church in commemoration of those "twenty-six martyrs" who died in the first Christian persecution under Hideyoshi. One day the foreign priest was surprised by a visit from some fifteen country folk, who said to him, when he appeared at the door, "The hearts of all of us here do not differ from yours." When he asked whence they came, they named their village, and added: "At home everybody is the same as we are." He tells us that the church was later visited by fifteen hundred people within two days, and that he learned of the existence of almost twice that many believers within the neighborhood; while in one particular place there were no less than a thousand Christian families.

The new government, therefore, doubtless inspired by the zealots of Mito, authorized a series of persecutions that reached their height in 1869. "Some of the Christians were tortured, beaten, or cast into prison. Thousands were sent into exile, being scattered among different provinces, and in many cases being forced to hard labor in the mines." "It is calculated," says a Roman Catholic writer, "that, between 1868 and 1873, from six thousand to eight thousand

Christians were torn from their families, deported, and subjected to cruel tortures, so
that nearly two thousand died in prison.''
The powers protested; but the United States
minister reports that ''after all our argu-
ments had been used, we were finally told by
Mr. Iwakura that this government rested
upon the Shintō faith, which taught the divinity of the Mikado; that the propagation of
the Christian faith and religion tended to
dispel that belief; and that consequently it
was the resolve of this government to resist
its propagation as they would resist the
advance of an invading army.''

Verbeck set himself steadfastly to secure
the repeal of the edicts against Christianity,
and it was through this very Iwa-
kura that he finally accomplished
his object, as the result of the
Great Embassy to Christendom, which he
himself inspired and directed.   Reasoning
that if the leaders of the nation could but be
induced to go abroad and see for themselves
the condition of Christian countries, they
would no longer proscribe a religion that had
wrought so wondrously for others, he submitted so early as 1869 a memorial to his former
pupils—but now the imperial councillors—

The Great
Embassy and
its Results.

that bore fruit two years later in the Great
Embassy that brought Japan to a position
in the front of the world-stage from which
she has never since receded, and also
achieved Verbeck's wish. For the great minister Iwakura himself headed this delegation,
and promptly telegraphed back to Japan in
accordance with his teacher's prediction and
desire, so that the edict-boards were at once
removed from the public highways, and the
principle of religious toleration was tacitly
established in their place.

This was in 1872,—a year noted for marvellous advance in the growth of the regener-
The Changes   ated empire. "The army, navy,
of 1872.   and civil service were entirely re-
constructed; the imperial mint at Ōsaka was
opened and a new coinage introduced; the
educational department, established in 1871,
largely extended its operations under an
enlightened minister, and the university was
firmly established at Tōkyō; the post-office
was organized, runners being employed, who,
by connections, could cover a hundred and
twenty-five miles a day; an industrial exhi-
bition was held in the sacred city of Kyōto;
and on June 12 the first railway in Japan
was opened from Tōkyō to Yokohama, a dis-

tance of eighteen miles." In the preceding year the abandoned daimiates had been superseded by a system of prefectures, responsible to a central cabinet in Tōkyō; and the despised *eta*, or pariahs of Japan, had been raised to the dignity of citizenship.

In all of these wonderful changes Verbeck had more or less influence. In recognition of his ability, the government next year made him adviser to the Imperial Japanese Senate. After serving five years in this unusual position of power, he was decorated by the Emperor with the great Order of the Rising Sun. In 1891 this "man without a country" was placed under the especial protection of the ægis of the Japanese empire, an honor without parallel in the entire history of Japan. And when, on March 10, 1898, he quietly fell asleep, the Emperor himself paid tribute to his obsequies, while military honors were observed above his grave, and an entire nation felt the touch of bereavement. This sketch has taken no account of his tremendous missionary labors as such. Only that side of his life is shown which is essential to an understanding of the forces that made "Young Japan." There were multitudes of foreign teachers who labored with him; but he stands as the leader of them all, the great tutor of the Japanese Revolution.

During his residence in Japan he saw the nation pass through all the throes inevitable The Progress upon her emergence from mediæ-of Reform. val hermitage sheer into the prominence of an actual world-power, which latter feat was eventually accomplished through her astonishing war with China. This landmark event in her history was preceded by a long series of struggles between the progressive and the conservative elements, wherein first one party would be momentarily successful and then the other; but the progressive element gained additional preponderance after each encounter, being strengthened even by apparent defeats.

The year 1873 continued a remarkable record in the introduction of foreign reforms. The European calendar was accepted, vaccination was introduced to do warfare against the ever prevalent scourge of small-pox, officials adopted the European dress, photography became a veritable fad, while the introduction of meat-eating showed that Buddhism was losing its hold upon the people in consequence of the official adoption of Shintō.

Certain of the powerful southern clansmen, as we have seen, did not relish the extreme liberalism of their colleagues at the helm, but they were none the less determined not to endure any criticism from outsiders. Korea had become most insolent since the revolution of 1868, neglecting to pay her immemorial tribute, and even venturing upon abusive letters in which she taunted Japan with slavish truckling to the "hairy barbarians" of the West. This was more than the dissatisfied conservatives could stand; so in 1874 the clansmen of Saga raised the old-time cry "On to Korea!" in opposition to the wisdom of the Tōkyō government, which perceived that for the present, at least, the country could not afford *The Saga Rebellion.* to dissipate its strength in a foreign war. The government troops came into collision with the southern soldiers, so intent were these upon their object, but the rebellion was quickly suppressed; and in the same year the government allowed these volcanic southerners to vent themselves upon the Chinese dependency of Formosa, whose cannibals had eaten a number of Japan's quasi vassals in

Loochoo. Formosa was punished, and Loo-
choo bound closer to Japan, while China at
Formosan   first threatened war, but afterwards
Expedition.   paid a grudging indemnity.

In the year 1875 the judiciary system was
carried on towards completion by the establishment of a court of cassation; courts of
first instance and courts of appeal being
already in existence. In the same year an
imperial edict created a senate, or house of
peers, which clearly foreshadowed a parliament. An eminent Japanese statesman
points out that ''thus, even at that early day,
a system was established in Japan resembling
the organization adopted by some western nations of co-ordinate governmental
branches, the executive, legislative, and judicial. This may be termed the first step
taken by the imperial government to pave the
way for the adoption of the constitutional
system.''

The lingering Korean unpleasantness was
happily settled in 1876, when the government
Treaty with   concluded a treaty which not only
Korea.   satisfied its own claims, but also
opened the last of the hermit nations to the
world. This year was also notable for the
adoption of Sunday as an official holiday,—

largely by reason of the fact that the numerous foreign employees residing in Japan
refused to labor on that day.

But in 1877 the Southern reactionaries
again made a stand, and with far more se-
rions consequences than before. Satsuma
Saigō, a veteran warrior, had not Rebellion.
experienced sufficient relief through his leadership of the Formosan expedition. He fret-
ted and fumed in the great principality of
Satsuma, having despised a seat in the pro-
foreign cabinet, against whom he was so vi-
ciously resentful that he and his compeers
began open preparations for war. When the
government learned that a great arsenal and
two large powder-mills were the scene of
busy activities in Satsuma, they sent thither
large bodies of imperial troops to seize these
stores. A war resulted, which lasted eight
months. The feeling in the south was so intense that even the women fought under
Saigō's banner. The Southern army num-
bered forty thousand men, who struggled
with desperate valor. But the insurrection
was finally suppressed, and with the surrender of Satsuma the main strength of the
opposition was broken.

In 1879, the government confirmed its hold

on Loochoo, in spite of the opposition of China, and Japan acquired her first foreign

Acquirement of Loochoo.

colony. The year was further notable through the visit of General Grant, which produced a most favorable impression, and strengthened the pro-foreign influence. The source of the government's troubles now shifted, and instead of having to oppose the conservatives, they found themselves unable to keep pace with the liberals. These were not even satisfied with the imperial promise, delivered in 1881, to establish a constitutional government nine years later. Political parties were formed, and the general unrest was intensified by troubles that arose in Korea. Japan succeeded in quelling the riots that raged in "the land of the morning calm;" but China seemed to become suspicious of the Mikado's designs, and roundly declared that Korea should not meet the fate of Loochoo. Chinese troops invested the country, and ill feeling was engendered that resulted in the Chino-Japanese war twelve

An Understanding with China.

years later. A nominal agreement was reached, however, in a treaty signed by China and Japan in 1885 whereby the two countries assumed a sort of joint protectorate over the land of the ironical name, exchanging a mutual pledge that in case of any future disturbances neither power should land troops in Korea without first giving notice to the other.

Events now rapidly moulded themselves towards the adoption of the promised constitution. A supreme court was established in 1884, a system of nobility was adopted on the European pattern, and English introduced as a branch of study in the common schools. In 1885 such sweeping reforms were made in the administration that it is known politically as the year of ''the great earthquake.'' Then it was that the present-day leaders came to the front, and especially Itō, who ranks to-day as the most powerful statesman of the East, and one of the few political leaders of the world. He had but just returned from Europe, where he had spent four years in the study of national constitutions, with a view to the preparation of the constitution promised by the Emperor. A veritable ''foreign fever'' now set in, which continued throughout several years. Everything from the West, including Christianity, was seized with an avidity that could hardly prove to be

Approach of Constitutional Government.

wholesome. Japanese ladies adopted the awkward European dress; the importation of Western dancing gave rise to grave scandals; the streets were a tangle of clumsy velocipedes; Japan became a land of monomaniacs.

But a reaction speedily followed. This was hastened by the refusal of Western nations to Foreign Fever allow a revision of the treaties. and Reaction. By the old treaties the government was bound not to impose a heavier customs tax than five per cent. on the importation of foreign merchandise, which greatly crippled the revenues. More than this, the treaties wounded the pride of Japan by requiring that all foreigners accused of misdemeanor should be tried by alien tribunals, albeit on Japanese territory. When the Japanese diplomatists failed in 1887 in their arduous efforts to secure an equitable revision, resentment was naturally aroused, and foreign friendship mistrusted. By the year 1889 the reaction in favor of native customs had reached its height, and murderous assaults were made by *sōshi* (the modern counterpart of the *rōnin*) not only upon foreigners, but also on certain pro-foreign statesmen. The assassins wrought costly havoc in the murder of Viscount Mori, who ranks with the martyred Ōkubo as a creator of the new Japan.

But the year was worthily signalized by the promulgation of the new constitution. On the very day that Mori was slain, The New —February 11, 1889,—the Em- Constitution. peror appeared in the throne-room, amid the assembled nobles of the realm and the representatives of all the great powers, to seal with impressive ceremonial the transition of Japan from an absolute to a constitutional monarchy. A year before he had appointed a special ''privy council,'' over whose deliberations he had presided, that the wisest thought of the realm might be spent in the testing of Itō's labors. Already the Marquis had had the assistance of a commission of three learned statesmen, who, during the several years that had succeeded his return from his studies in Europe, gave themselves under his presidency to a careful preparation of the draft.* Thus the entire period that had intervened since the Emperor's promise, had

* The author is indebted to a member of this commission, Baron Kaneko, for valuable information bearing on this subject. See the Century Magazine for July, 1904.

been occupied with the most painstaking care in the preparation of Japan's "magna charta." The instrument is in every way worthy. The late James G. Blaine pronounced it to be structurally perfect; Herbert Spencer and James Bryce have called it an extraordinary success.

The constitution is strong in its simplicity. It contains only the fundamental principles *Its Simplicity.* of state, while matters of detail are embodied in supplemental laws. Its seventy-six articles are confined to "the prerogatives of the Emperor; the rights and duties of the people; the powers of parliament; the powers and duties of ministers of state and judiciary and finance." The entire instrument is the logical outcome of Mutsuhito's "charter oath," delivered in 1869.* It is given herewith, in a translation effected at Johns Hopkins University in the year of its adoption.

THE CONSTITUTION OF JAPAN.

HAVING, by virtue of the glories of Our Ancestors, ascended the throne of a lineal succession unbroken for ages eternal; desiring to promote the welfare of, and to give development to the moral and intellectual fac-

---

* See page 221.

ulties of Our beloved subjects, the very same that have been favoured with the benevolent care and affectionate vigilance of Our Ancestors; and hoping to maintain the prosperity of the State, in concert with Our people and with their support, We hereby promulgate, in pursuance of Our Imperial Rescript of the 14th day of the 10th month of the 14th year of Meiji, a fundamental law of State, to exhibit the principles by which We are to be guided in Our conduct, and to point out to what Our descendants and Our subjects and their descendants are to forever conform. The rights of sovereignty of the State, We have inherited from Our Ancestors, and We shall bequeath them to Our descendants. Neither We nor they shall in future fail to wield them, in accordance with the provisions of the Constitution hereby granted. We now declare to respect and protect the security of the rights and the property of Our people, and to secure to them the complete enjoyment of the same, within the extent of the provisions of the present Constitution and of the law. The Imperial Diet shall first be convoked for the 23d year of Meiji, and the time of its opening shall be the date, when the present Constitution comes into force. When in the future it may become necessary to amend any of the provisions of the present Constitution, We or Our successors shall assume the initiative right, and submit a project for the same to the Imperial Diet. The Imperial Diet shall pass its vote upon it, according to the conditions imposed by the present Constitution, and in no other wise shall Our descendants or Our subjects be permitted to attempt any alteration thereof. Our Ministers of State, on Our behalf, shall be held responsible for the carrying out of the present Constitution, and Our present and future subjects shall assume the duty of allegiance to the present Constitution. (His Imperial Majesty's Sign-Manual.) The 11th day of the 2nd month of the 22nd year of Meiji. (Countersigned by Ministers.)

CHAPTER I. (EMPEROR.)

ARTICLE I. The Empire of Japan shall be reigned over by and governed by a line of Emperors unbroken for ages eternal.

ARTICLE II. The Imperial Throne shall be succeeded to by Imperial descendants, according to the provisions of the Imperial House Law.

ARTICLE III. The Emperor is sacred and inviolable.

ARTICLE IV. The Emperor is head of the Empire, combining in Himself the rights of sovereignty, and exercising them, according to the provisions of the present Constitution.

ARTICLE V. The Emperor exercises the legislative power with the consent of the Imperial Diet.

ARTICLE VI. The Emperor gives sanction to the laws, and orders them to be promulgated and executed.

ARTICLE VII. The Emperor convokes the Imperial Diet, opens, closes, and prorogues it, and dissolves the House of Representatives.

ARTICLE VIII. The Emperor, in consequence of an urgent necessity to maintain public safety or to avert public calamities, issues, when the Imperial Diet is not sitting, Imperial Ordinances in the place of law. Such Imperial Ordinances are to be laid before the Imperial Diet at its next session, and when the Diet does not approve the said Ordinances, the Government shall declare them to be invalid for the future.

ARTICLE IX. The Emperor issues, or causes to be

issued, the ordinances necessary for the carrying out of the laws, or for the maintenance of the public peace and order, and for the promotion of the welfare of the subjects. But no ordinance shall in any way alter any of the existing laws.

ARTICLE X. The Emperor determines the organization of the different branches of the administration, and the salaries of all civil and military officers, and appoints and dismisses the same. Exceptions especially provided for in the present Constitution or in other laws, shall be in accordance with the respective provisions (bearing thereon).

ARTICLE XI. The Emperor has the supreme command of the Army and Navy.

ARTICLE XII. The Emperor determines the organization and peace-standing of the Army and Navy.

ARTICLE XIII. The Emperor declares war, makes peace, and concludes treaties.

ARTICLE XIV. The Emperor proclaims the law of siege. The conditions and effects of the law of siege shall be determined by law.

ARTICLE XV. The Emperor confers titles of nobility, rank, orders, and other marks of honor.

ARTICLE XVI. The Emperor orders amnesty, pardon, commutation of punishment, and rehabilitation.

ARTICLE XVII. A Regency shall be instituted in conformity with the provisions of the Imperial House Law. The Regent shall exercise the powers appertaining to the Emperor in His name.

CHAPTER II. (SUBJECTS.)

ARTICLE XVIII. The conditions for being a Japanese subject shall be determined by law.

ARTICLE XIX. Japanese subjects may, according to qualifications determined in law or ordinances, be appointed to civil or military offices equally, and may fill any other offices.

ARTICLE XX. Japanese subjects are amenable to service in the Army or Navy, according to the provisions of law.

ARTICLE XXI. Japanese subjects are amenable to the duty of paying taxes, according to the provisions of law.

ARTICLE XXII. Japanese subjects shall have the liberty of abode and of changing the same within the limits of law.

ARTICLE XXIII. No Japanese subject shall be arrested, detained, tried, or punished, unless according to law.

ARTICLE XXIV. No Japanese subject shall be deprived of his right of being tried by the judges determined by law.

ARTICLE XXV. Except in the cases provided for in the law, the house of no Japanese shall be entered or searched without his consent.

ARTICLE XXVI. Except in the cases mentioned in the law, the secrecy of the letters of every Japanese subject shall remain inviolate.

ARTICLE XXVII. The right of property of every Japanese subject shall remain inviolate. Measures necessary to be taken for the public benefit shall be provided for by law.

ARTICLE XXVIII. Japanese subjects shall, within limits not prejudicial to peace and order, and not antagonistic to their duties as subjects, enjoy freedom of religious belief.

ARTICLE XXIX. Japanese subjects shall, within the limits of law, enjoy the liberty of speech, writing, publication, public meetings, and associations.

ARTICLE XXX. Japanese subjects may present petitions, by observing the proper forms of respect, and by complying with the rules specially provided for the same.

ARTICLE XXXI. The provisions contained in the present Chapter shall not affect the exercise of the powers appertaining to the Emperor in times of war or in cases of national emergency.

ARTICLE XXXII. Each and every one of the provisions contained in the preceding articles of the present Chapter, that are not in conflict with the laws or rules and discipline of the Army and Navy, shall apply to the officers and men of the Army and Navy.

CHAPTER III. (DIET.)

ARTICLE XXXIII. The Imperial Diet shall consist of two Houses, a House of Peers and a House of Representatives.

ARTICLE XXXIV. The House of Peers shall, in accordance with the Ordinance concerning the House of Peers, be composed of members of the Imperial Family, of the orders of nobility, and of those persons who have been nominated thereto by the Emperor.

ARTICLE XXXV. The House of Representatives shall be composed of Members elected by the people according to the provisions of the Law of Election.

ARTICLE XXXVI. No one can at one and the same time be a member of both Houses.

ARTICLE XXXVII. Every law requires the consent of the Imperial Diet.

ARTICLE XXXVIII. Both Houses shall vote on projects of law submitted to it by the Government, and may respectively initiate projects of law.

ARTICLE XXXIX. A Bill, which has been rejected by either the one or the other of the Houses, shall not be again brought in during the same session.

ARTICLE XL. Both Houses can make representations to the Government, as to laws or upon any other subject. When, however, such representations are not accepted, they cannot be made a second time during the same session.

ARTICLE XLI. The Imperial Diet shall be convoked every year.

ARTICLE XLII. A session of the Imperial Diet shall last during three months. In case of necessity, the duration of a session may be prolonged by the Imperial Order.

ARTICLE XLIII. When urgent necessity arises, an extraordinary session may be convoked, in addition to the ordinary one. The duration of an extraordinary session shall be determined by Imperial Order.

ARTICLE XLIV. The opening, closing, prolongation of session, and prorogation of the Imperial Diet, shall be effected simultaneously for both Houses. In case the House of Representatives has been ordered to dissolve, the House of Peers shall at the same time be prorogued.

ARTICLE XLV. When the House of Representatives has been ordered to dissolve, members shall be caused by Imperial Order to be newly elected, and the new House shall be convoked within five months from the day of dissolution.

ARTICLE XLVI. No debate can be opened and no vote can be taken in either House of the Imperial Diet, unless not less than one-third of the whole numbers of the members thereof be present.

ARTICLE XLVII. Votes shall be taken in both Houses by absolute majority. In case of a tie-vote the president shall have the casting vote.

ARTICLE XLVIII. The deliberations of both Houses shall be held in· public. The deliberations may, however, upon demand of the Government or by resolution of the House, be held in secret sitting.

ARTICLE XLIX. Both Houses of the Imperial Diet may respectively present addresses to the Emperor.

ARTICLE L. Both Houses may receive petitions presented by subjects.

ARTICLE LI. Both Houses may enact, besides what is provided for in the present Constitution and in the Law of the Houses, rules necessary for the management of their internal affairs.

ARTICLE LII. No member of either House shall be held responsible outside the respective Houses, for any opinion uttered or any vote given in the House. ' When, however, a member himself has given publicity to his opinions by public speech, by documents in printing or in writing, or by any similar means he shall, in the matter, be amenable to the general law.

ARTICLE LIII. The members of both Houses shall, during the session, be freed from arrest, unless with the consent of the House, except in cases of flagrant delicts, or of offences connected with a state of internal commotion or with a foreign trouble.

ARTICLE LIV. The Ministers of State and the Delegates of the Government may, at any time, take seats and speak in either House.

CHAPTER IV. (MINISTRY.)

ARTICLE LV. The respective Ministers of State shall give their advice to the Emperor, and be responsible for it. All Laws, Imperial Ordinances, and Imperial Rescripts of whatever kind, that relate to the affairs of the State, require the countersignature of a Minister of State.

ARTICLE LVI. The Privy Council shall, in accordance with the provisions for the organization of the Privy Council, deliberate upon important matters of State, when they have been consulted by the Emperor.

CHAPTER V. (JUDICIARY.)

ARTICLE LVII. The Judicature shall be exercised by the Courts of Law according to law, in the name of the Emperor. The organization of the Courts of Law shall be determined by law.

ARTICLE LVIII. The judges shall be appointed from among those, who possess proper qualifications according to law. No judge shall be deprived of his position, unless by way of criminal sentence or disciplinary punishment. Rules for disciplinary punishment shall be determined by law.

ARTICLE LIX. Trials and judgments of a Court shall be conducted publicly. When, however, there exists any fear that such publicity may be prejudicial to peace and order, or to the maintenance of public morality, the public trial may be suspended by provision of law or by the decision of the Court of Law.

ARTICLE LX. All matters that fall within the competency of a special Court, shall be specially provided for by law.

ARTICLE LXI. No suit at law, which relates to rights alleged to have been infringed by the legal measures of the executive authorities, and which shall come within the competency of the Court of Administrative Litigation specially established by law, shall be taken cognizance of by a Court of Law.

CHAPTER VI. (FINANCE.)

ARTICLE LXII. The imposition of a new tax or the modification of the rates (of an existing one) shall be determined by law. However, all such administrative fees or other revenue having the nature of compensation shall not fall within the category of the above clause. The raising of national loans and the contracting of other liabilities to the charge of the national treasury, except those that are provided in the Budget, shall require the consent of the Imperial Diet.

ARTICLE LXIII. The taxes levied at present shall, in so far as they are not remodelled by new law, be collected according to the old system.

ARTICLE LXIV. The expenditure and revenue of the State require the consent of the Imperial Diet by means of an annual Budget. Any and all expenditures overpassing the appropriations set forth in the Titles and Paragraphs of the Budget, shall subsequently require the approbation of the Imperial Diet.

ARTICLE LXV. The Budget shall be first laid before the House of Representatives.

ARTICLE LXVI. The expenditures of the Imperial House shall be defrayed every year out of the National Treasury, according to the present fixed amount for the same, and shall not require the consent thereto of the

Imperial Diet, except in case an increase thereof is found necessary.

ARTICLE LXVII. Those already fixed expenditures based by the Constitution upon the powers appertaining to the Emperor, and such expenditures as may have arisen by the effect of the law, or that appertain to the legal obligations of the Government, shall be neither rejected nor reduced by the Imperial Diet, without the concurrence of the Government.

ARTICLE LXVIII. In order to meet special requirements, the Government may ask the consent of the Imperial Diet to a certain amount as a Continuing Expenditure Fund, for a previously fixed number of years.

ARTICLE LXIX. In order to supply deficiencies which are unavoidable, in the Budget, and to meet requirements unprovided for in the same, a Reserve Fund shall be provided in the Budget.

ARTICLE LXX. When the Imperial Diet cannot be convoked, owing to the external or the internal condition of the country, in case of urgent need for the maintenance of public safety, the Government may take all necessary financial measures, by means of an Imperial Ordinance. In the case mentioned in the preceding clause, the matter shall be submitted to the Imperial Diet at its next session, and its approbation shall be obtained thereto.

ARTICLE LXXI. When the Imperial Diet has not voted on the Budget, or when the Budget has not been brought into actual existence, the Government shall carry out the Budget of the preceding year.

ARTICLE LXXII. The final account of the expenditures and revenue of the State shall be verified and confirmed by the Board of Audit, and it shall be submitted by the Government to the Imperial Diet, together with the report of verification of said Board. The organization and competency of the Board of Audit shall be determined by law separately.

CHAPTER VII. (RULES.)

ARTICLE LXXIII. When it has become necessary in the future to amend the provisions of the present Constitution, a project to that effect shall be submitted to the Imperial Diet by Imperial Order. In the above case, neither House can open the debate, unless not less than two-thirds of the whole number of Members are present, and no amendment can be passed unless a majority of not less than two-thirds of the Members present is obtained.

ARTICLE LXXIV. No modification of the Imperial House Law shall be required to be submitted to the deliberation of the Imperial Diet. No provision of the present Constitution can be modified by the Imperial House Law.

ARTICLE LXXV. No modification can be introduced into the Constitution, or into the Imperial House Law, during the time of a Regency.

ARTICLE LXXVI. Existing legal enactments, such as laws, regulations, Ordinances, or by whatever names they may be called, shall, so far as they do not conflict with the present Constitution, continue in force. All existing contracts or orders, that entail obligations upon the Government, and that are connected with expenditure shall come within the scope of Art. LXVII.

This constitution is a remarkable example of the eclectic methods whereby Japan has built up all of her modern national structures. The imperialist features are borrowed from the Germans, while the theory of equal rights is taken from the English. The house of peers is moulded on the Prussian model, while the house of representatives savors of America and France. The experience of the "Long Parliament" in England taught the advisability of guaranteeing to members the right of free speech, while from Bismarck was acquired an important hint which enables the ministry to checkmate any obstreperous diet that might refuse to pass the budget,—"when the Imperial Diet has not voted on the Budget, the Government shall carry out the Budget of the preceding year." Thus the wily empire-builders learned lessons from this country and that, making for themselves a constitution equal to that of any other country in the world. A shrewd historical scholar has recently said that "if Nicholas and his council of state had the insight and the moral courage of Mutsuhito and the statesmen of the Japanese Restoration, they could by a similar policy increase the power, the safety, and the development of Russia in an almost miraculous degree.''

The way had been paved for the sessions of the Diet by the establishment of prefectural assemblies so long ago as 1879. These correspond in some degree

The New Diet.

at least to our State legislatures, each prefect being administered by a governor (appointed, however, from Tōkyō), who submits the fiscal proposals. Ten years of actual practice in local deliberative assemblies qualified the members of the new Diet for their more responsible positions, and thus the chief function of the prefectural assemblies is doubtless that of a fitting school. The first session of the Diet (held in the winter of 1890–1891) was somewhat stormy, however, and certain subsequent sessions have sometimes reached an extremity of disturbance that have made scholars tremble for the future of constitutional government in Japan. But Baron Kaneko now points out that since twenty sessions have been held without doing violence to constitutional rights or restrictions, ''it can be justly claimed that constitutional government has passed the experimental stage in Japan and has become an integral part of the body politic.''

The wording of this instrument is ambiguous with reference to the responsibility of the ministry. Until the year 1898, it was claimed that their sole accountability was to the Emperor, which means that they accounted to themselves. In that year, however, a great victory was gained in behalf of a more popular government by establishing the responsibility of the ministry to the Diet.

The house of peers is composed partly of hereditary members, partly of those who are The Two nominated or elected. The higher Houses. nobility hold seats for life, and so do such men of ability as may be nominated to office by the Emperor. Those who are elected serve for a term of seven years. The house of representatives consists of about three hundred members, who must be at least thirty years of age and pay national taxes amounting to at least fifteen *yen* ($7.50). Their term of service is four years. The electorate is limited by a property qualification, so that the voters of Japan form only about two per cent. of the whole population.

In spite of the numerous stormy sessions of the Diet, and the frequent convulsions in the ministry, the country has always acted as one man where foreign relations were involved. This was notably true in connection with the Chinese war. Up to the declaration of hostilities, Marquis Itō had been the target for continual and violent attacks on the floor of the house of representatives, so that, every bill of his having been defeated, he twice took advantage of his position as premier and dissolved the Diet. It was freely predicted in the West that the internal dissensions of Japan would make her an easy prey in the clutches of her huge angry neighbor. But when war was actually declared, the Diet rallied to the support of the Marquis, and one of his associates informs us that "if it had not been for the Parliament in Japan, we could never have fought the Japanese-Chinese war to a successful conclusion."

The superficial story of this war may be told in very few words. It will be remembered that in 1884, after Japan had The Chinese quelled the murderous riots that War. raged in "the land of the morning calm," a treaty was signed with China whereby the agreement was reached that neither power should in future send troops to Korea without first giving due notice to the other. Japan showed great generosity in signing such a

17

treaty with China in view of her far larger suzerain rights, and in the face of the incessant Celestial bickerings. But the treaty was signed; and whatever may be said of the individual Japanese honesty, the government itself has always been scrupulously honest in all of its international promises. Not so with China. When, in 1894, riots amounting almost to domestic war broke out in the wretchedly misgoverned country, China very promptly attempted to strengthen her Korean pretensions by sending thither a large body of troops, contemptuously ignoring the agreement of giving previous notice to Japan. Japan also thereupon sent troops to Korea, but only after notice had been served upon China. The proximity of the turbulent little country, and its power to awaken dissensions in Japan, made it imperative for the Japanese government to undertake some measures that might insure Korean reforms and bring about a consequent enduring peace. Japan, therefore, generously ignoring the contemptuous action of her treaty associate, proposed that they should jointly undertake the introduction of Korean reforms; but added, with commendable firmness, that if China should not co-operate, she would feel compelled to proceed alone. China not only refused to co-operate, but demanded that Japan should withdraw her troops. Japan, however, sent over more soldiers, and prepared for the introductions of reforms. The Korean king (who is now "emperor") heartily seconded this movement, but the powerful and riotous "Ming" faction, who had been the immediate cause of all of the troubles, intrigued with China and assaulted the escort of the Japanese minister. Shortly thereafter, on the attempt of the Chinese to land more troops in Korea, Japanese war-vessels attacked the Chinese transports, and actual hostilities began. On the first day of August, 1894, the Chinese emperor issued a formal declaration of war, wherein he claimed that "Korea has been our tributary for the last two hundred years," and derided the Japanese as "pygmies." "We have always followed the paths of philanthropy and perfect justice," the declaration continues, "while the pygmies, on the other hand, have broken all the laws of nations and treaties, which it passes our patience to bear with. Hence we command Li Hung Chang to give strict orders to our various armies to hasten with all speed to root the pygmies out of their lairs.''

The event proved, however, that the ''pygmies'' possessed a strength out of all proportion to their size. The country rallied to the support of Marquis Itō's vigorous policy, and Europe's almost universal feeling of pity for the ''little brown people'' was swiftly changed to amazed admiration. After a brief but thrilling campaign, the Chinese emperor commanded Li Hung Chang to go peacefully into the ''lairs'' of these ''pygmies'' and arrange for a temporary armistice. An irresponsible *sōshi*— Japan's noxious inheritance from feudalism —complicated the situation severely by an assault on the Chinese ambassador at Shimonoseki (March 24, 1895). The writer of this volume was in Shimonoseki at the time, and can bear personal witness to the intense grief into which this act plunged the Japanese people. They felt that their honor had been outraged, and this for the second time in five years; * and that the civilized world might now repudiate their comity, on account of this

The Peace Negotiations.

* The other occasion was in 1891, when the visiting Czarevitch was assaulted and almost slain.

irresponsible assassin. The Emperor immediately volunteered an unconditional armistice, so that the event really hastened the end
of the war. On the 17th of April, 1895, a
peace treaty was concluded at Shimonoseki,
which included the following terms: China
recognizes the independence of Korea; China
cedes to Japan the Liaotung peninsula, the
island of Formosa, and the Pescadores
group; China pays an indemnity of three
hundred million *yen;* ratifications of this
treaty shall be exchanged within three weeks.
In the negotiation of this treaty, China had
the personal counsel of the distinguished
American diplomatist, John W. Foster; and
there is no sign that the terms were regarded
by her as illiberal. But as soon as the treaty
had been ratified, there came a most startling
interference. Russia, supported by Germany
and France, suddenly appeared   Russia's
upon the scene with the demand   Interference.
that the Liaotung peninsula should not be
ceded to Japan, on the ground that "such
permanent possession would be detrimental
to the peace of the Orient, and a menace to
Korea and China." Japan was placed in a
most humiliating position; it would have
been infinitely kinder had the powers inter-

posed before the ratification of the treaty, since its terms were perfectly well known. As it was, the sanity and self-control of the Japanese stood this severest of tests. Realizing the futility of opposing such a formidable array of force, the Emperor issued a rescript on the 10th of May in which he accepted the disinterested professions of the powers at their face value, and surrendered the chief prize of the war for the sake of "an enduring peace."

Such is the superficial story of the Chino-Japanese war, told in its briefest outline. Japan's Power Recognized. The effect of the victory, in spite of its humiliating sequel, was to establish Japan's prestige among the nations as a power that has to be reckoned with. An American resident of Tōkyō contributed to the *Japan Mail* verses entitled "The Great Powers to Japan," wherein they are represented as shouting:

> "*Salve* Japan!　We seven, the sovereign Powers,
> Greet thee compeer; inscrol thy name with ours,—
> United States, Great Britain, Germany,
> France, Russia, Austro-Hungary,
> And Italy.　Henceforth the world-estate
> We share with thee—Japan the Great."

It may have been an accident, but the first victories of Japan in her war with China were immediately followed by the revision of the treaties for which she had hitherto striven in vain. In September, 1894, Great Britain led the way, to be followed shortly by other nations, in an agreement that after the lapse of five years Japan should be granted both tariff and judicial autonomy; while on the other hand foreigners should be allowed to travel or reside in any part of the empire without the need of a special passport. Thus the humiliation to which the country was subjected by Russia was offset to a certain extent by the significant friendship of England,—Russia's traditional foe.

It is now necessary for us to look far beneath the surface of this Chinese war, in order to understand the greater war which is its sequel, and also to gain a hint, in passing, as to the meaning of the strange Chinese "Boxer" uprising in 1900, and of the more recent Anglo-Japanese Alliance. To this end, we must imagine ourselves in northern Manchuria just two hundred years ago, watching the advancing tides of that great Slavonian invasion which has poured steadily over the continent of Asia until at last it beats upon the ocean for an outlet, only to find itself confronted and confined by the opposing billows of the little Sea of Japan. Two centuries ago Russia had already acquired the greater part of Siberia from the Tatars; but this must needs prove Russia and only a barren conquest unless she Manchuria. could find some outlet for her vast new territory in unfrozen southern seas. Manchuria lies between Siberia and this coveted outlet, the two territories finding a natural dividing line in the sinuous Amur River, which describes a great overturned S as it runs its course of nigh three thousand miles from the interior to the Gulf of Saghalien. Had we taken our stand in northern Manchuria two hundred years ago, we should have seen the thoughtful Russians already making encroachments towards the south, crossing the Amur River, and erecting two forts south of it. But the Chinese were suspicious, and the great arsenal town of Kirin was built to defend northern Manchuria, while they sent courageous troops to drive the Russians back again over the Amur River. These doughty Celestial soldiers captured the Russian forts, whose garrisons were conveyed

as prisoners to Pekin, where they still form a
Russian colony of greater use to the Czar
than a hundred garrisons of soldiers.   For
they represent the militant spirit of Russia,
and they live in the Chinese capital.

In the year 1847, Count Nicholas Muravief
became governor of eastern Siberia, under
whose bold administration Russia   Muravief.
made great strides southward.   His
most important step was to take advantage
of the situation wherein China found herself
ten years after he had been made governor.
Through the mediation of the colony in
Peking, China was caused to believe that she
owed to Russia her deliverance from the
Anglo-French occupation; and to present a
token of gratitude in the shape of a great slice
of the Manchurian coast, by which Russia
gained territory larger than the State of
Texas, and advanced ten degrees to the south.
At the base of this great Ussuri   Vladivostok.
region a vast fortress was imme-
diately erected, which received the appro-
priate name of Vladivostok, meaning ''dominator of the East.''   This was in 1861.

But there were important geographical
reasons why Vladivostok could not dominate
the East.   A glance at a map will show that

the entire coast-line of the Ussuri region, together with the eastern shore of Korea, is completely hemmed in by Japan. Beginning with the island of Saghalien, a great sea-wall bends around this central coast of Asia, which is thus shut off from the Pacific and confined by the waters of the Sea of Japan. When Japan awakened from her age-long torpor, Russia seemed on the point of realizing the true situation, and succeeded (1875) in buying the north end of the sea-wall—Saghalien— in exchange for the Kurile Islands. But this by no means relieved the Russian difficulties. The actual approaches to Vladivostok are the two straits that lie at the northern and southern extremities of Japan; only through these doors as an outlet can Vladivostok reach the Pacific. Russia had attempted to seize command of the southern strait immediately upon the creation of the "dominator;" but England had blocked her designs. The only ideal outlet for Russia is afforded by the coast of Korea.

Muravief perceived that the colossal plans of Russia in the East could only be accomplished by closer connections with home. He therefore conceived the idea of a great continental railroad, which should

The Great Railway.

link the far-off European capital with its ambitious Asiatic frontier. The two ends of the
railroad were first completed, and Russia
meanwhile played a silent hand in Eastern
politics. The little colony at Pekin was not
forgotten. The bickerings of China about
Formosa and Korea are more easily understood when we keep that little colony in mind.
But China agreed to a joint protectorate with
Japan over Korea in 1885, and the bickerings
seemed about to cease. In the very next year,
however, Great Britain unearthed a Russian
plot to make Korea a protectorate
of the Czar,—a situation which   Russian Plots.
continually reminds us of the fable about the
cat, the two monkeys, and the cheese. England finally exacted a promise from the Russian government that it should never attempt
the absorption of Korea.

But the Czar urged the hastening of the
railroad, and the sinuous Amur River was in
the way. It was still the boundary line between Russia and Manchuria, so that Russia,
if confined to her own territory, would have
to bend all around the northern shore of the
enormous overturned S before she could run
her rails down through the Ussuri region to
Vladivostok. It would be infinitely easier to

construct the road by a bee-line driven through Manchuria! So Russia, with her accustomed stupendous audacity, came to China in 1893 with a proposal "to construct an extension of the Trans-Siberian Railway, to be known as the Chinese Eastern Railway, by the short cut across Manchuria."

But Marquis Itō was watching from afar. He foresaw, as any one may clearly see now,

Itō's Vigilance. that to build a railway through Manchuria would be to control that immense territory, since this is the era of conquests by railroads; that the next step of the Russian advance would be planted in Korea; and that "Korea in Russian hands would be a dagger pointed at the heart of Japan." The short-sighted Japanese Diet at first opposed his warlike spirit, but Russia overplayed her game in China, so that Japan was apparently driven into war against her will, as we have seen.

While this war was at its height, the great Czar Alexander III. passed away. For forty

The Young Czar. years fortune had favored Russia with mighty emperors; but absolute despotism is an awful power to intrust to the chances of heredity. Russia had been fortunate for forty years, and her wonderful growth during that period is chiefly due to the remarkable strength of her rulers; but what of this stripling of twenty-six, reputed to be good-natured but feeble, as he suddenly ascends to dizzy heights of power? Among other things, what of his relation to Japan? He had been severely wounded while travelling through the country in 1891,—did he mistake the courteous humiliation of his hosts for weakness, and their noble shame for an ignoble cowardice? Would he despise and underrate Japan, as the Chinese had done to their cost? Nine days after the death of Alexander III., the *Weekly Mail*, a powerful British journal published in Japan, uttered words of a deep significance when read in the light of the present: "The untimely death of such a ruler when twenty or thirty years of his beneficent sovereignty might reasonably have been expected, is a universal calamity. . . . The succession of a youth of twenty-six to the Russian Throne is an event fraught with the gravest contingencies."

Meanwhile, the war hastened to its end. We have seen that the wisdom of Marquis Itō caused him to specify the cession of the Liao-tung peninsula to Japan as the most important item in the treaty of peace. This would not necessarily have prevented the building of the Chinese Eastern railroad, but it would have made Japan able to protect her Korean interests, for Port Arthur, at the tip of the peninsula, is the key to the Korean situation. Russia, however, intervened, having by some means persuaded France and Germany to unite with her in a protest against a situation "which would endanger the peace of the Orient, besides threatening the integrity of Korea and China"—as they declared. But no sooner had Japan been forced to acquiesce, than Russia obtained from the Chinese government permission to build her short-line railway through Manchuria, as a reward for the services she had rendered in enabling China to keep the Liaotung peninsula.

Russian Inconsistency.

Three years later (1898), a missionary tragedy was turned into an international farce. Two German missionaries having been murdered by a Chinese mob, the German government demanded as indemnity a portion of the province of Shantung. Russia immediately followed with the plea that this cession to Germany "disturbed the balance of power," and that mat-

Strange Stratagems.

ters might only be equalized if she should be granted a lease of the very peninsula from which she had driven Japan three years before! China, of course, weakly consented, and Russia then proceeded to build a branch of her railroad from Harbin straight down to Port Arthur, where she planted powerful guns upon the heights, after filling the town with her soldiers, and after having closed the harbor to all vessels except her own. Where now were Russia's protestations of concern for "the enduring peace of the Orient, and the integrity of Korea and China"?

A greater tragedy brought the farce to its climax in 1900. That was the year of the terrible Boxer War. Russia took advantage of that massacre to gar- **Boxer War.** rison all Manchuria with her troops, as a "temporary" measure of protection. She had invested large interests in Manchuria, and must needs look after them. But when the time came for her to withdraw her troops, she insolently increased them. Manchuria became an enormous Russian garrison, and advances were stealthily made on Korea. Meanwhile, Japan had been preparing for the impending crisis. She saw that she must face an issue of life and death; for, if Korea should once fall into the hands of Russia, "there would thus be planted almost within cannon-range of her shores a power of enormous strength and insatiable ambition," which would most certainly reach out just a little farther and seize the rich prize of **Japan's Danger.** Japan, filled as it is with splendid harbors and forming a magnificent outpost for the coast of the Orient. Japan had been preparing for the struggle, but her elder statesmen hoped that it might not come. She had doubled her army and trebled her navy, but her leaders strove to hold her strength in leash. They realized the enormous disparity of forces, and the terrible possibilities which a struggle might involve. In July, 1903, they approached Russia with the respectful request for a treaty. Negotiations were begun upon a perfectly reasonable basis,—Japan offering to acknowledge the **The War Opens.** interests of Russia in Manchuria, but insisting that Korea be left free. Russia delayed and trifled to an extent that is almost incredible. The fact is, she despised Japan. As her greatest leaders now confess, she never dreamed that Japan would fight. "Her people are but pygmies, a little monkey race of islanders." To overawe these "monkey-faced men," fresh armies were sent to Manchuria, and also a great naval fleet. Finally, on the 8th of February, 1904, having exhausted the resources of peace, the little agile country struck its first blow, and electrified the world.

The English Alliance? It was perfected a year or two before, not only because England is wise, but also because England believes in fair play. Its chief de- *Importance of the War.* clared object is Chinese and Korean integrity; but Great Britain also clearly perceives that in this tremendous drama which is being played in the world-theatre to-day, far larger interests are concerned than the political interests of two isolated nations. It is a war of principles, and universal history will be affected by its issues. The subtle East and the open-handed West are fighting their struggle for mastery,—Russia coming out of the East, Tatar to the very bone, while Japan is the sole hope of the West in Asia. As for Christianity, if Russia be Christian, then the less we have of that religion the better. Two tides are crashing thunderously together off the coasts of Japan to-day. The one has rolled across the steppes

18

of Asia dark with barbarism, the other meets it from the Pacific, bright with light. It is despotism against liberty, the past against the future, night against day, wrong against right. And an eloquent writer, foreseeing this war, has said: "I look to see the Japanese Revolution succeed against the Russian Tradition; that is to say, I look for justice in history; I expect to find that truth is its own ultimate strength and vindication. I anticipate that those standards which civilization has agreed to regard as the higher shall also be proven the stronger. And this even if—as is possible—the tonnage and the battalions of the Tradition should for a time succeed, as have its lies and its brigandage. And remember that all that the Revolution asks of the Tradition is toleration and respect for its clear rights."

Before passing to the concluding chapter of our story of "Young Japan" it may be well to glance at the organization of The Japanese Army. that remarkable army and navy to whose brilliant efficiency it is chiefly due that a new sun has risen above the horizon of history—for Japan, the "Sunrise Land," has fulfilled the prophecy of her name. It was in that wonderful year of changes, A.D. 1872, that the army and navy of the new Japan were organized. Being thoroughly convinced that Western nations could teach them somewhat in the matter of military effectiveness, the new Sat-Chō government surrounding the Emperor and holding the reins of rule concluded from the investigations of their world-touring embassy that France could furnish the best drill-masters. French military advisers were therefore employed for the army, but these were afterwards supplanted by Germans. An effective modern army resulted in a surprisingly short time, simply because the soldiers of old Japan were surpassingly brave and loyal through immemorial drill, with a native alertness and thoroughness that gave them immediate grasp of new forms, and a self-control that adds the summit-touch to soldiery.* Conscription laws of the most radical character supply fresh material from the flower of the youth of the land every year, at the rate of forty thousand or more. In the rigid weeding-out processes—for the most stringent mental and physical tests are in practice—those who are rejected as fighting-men are sent with the

---

* See page 148.

army as transporters. The father of the army is the Marquis Yamagata, who has now (at the age of sixty-six) attained to the rank of field-marshal. In fifteen years it has grown from an enlistment of 228,848 men to a strength of 508,268, all told—on a peace footing.* There are six chief military stations, evenly distributed throughout the empire.

Baron Yamamoto, the present minister of the navy, is to this branch of the service what The Japanese Yamagata has been to the army. In Navy. 1902, against the most vigorous opposition, he induced parliament to undertake the construction of six first-class battleships within the next ten years, so that Japan has not yet approached the limit of her naval expansion. It was Great Britain that supervised the beginnings, sending out a small school of instructors so long ago as 1867, under the Shōgunate, and a larger one in 1873, after the Restoration. Dockyard work, however, was committed to the direction of the French. The principal dockyards are at Yokosuka, in the Gulf of Tōkyō; but there

* The figures are for the years 1888 and 1903, respectively.

are others at Kure, in the Inland Sea; Sasebo, near Nagasaki; Maizuru, on the west coast; and Mororan, in the island of Yezo. There are four ship-building concerns where steel-frame steamers can be constructed; and some idea of the rapidity with which Japan is mastering this difficult industry can be gained from the fact that out of the nine and a half million tonnage of steam-vessels passing annually through her ports, fully three million are of native construction. At the beginning of the war with Russia the naval fleet included six first-class battleships, eight armored cruisers, and fourteen protected cruisers. At the close of the first year's fighting three of these vessels had been lost, while the Russian eastern fleet, of equal fighting strength in the beginning, had been practically swept from the seas.

The principal naval academy is at Etajimà, an island of the beautiful Inland Sea. Applicants must be at least sixteen years of age, and are subjected to rigid examination. The training is strict in the extreme, and *jiū-jutsu* is the favorite physical exercise. The average age of the navy is the lowest in the world, as is also the average height: no one over twenty years of age is accepted for enlistment, and the average stature is only five feet and four inches.

It is a theory that "in Japan every subject has a chance for a commission in the imperial The Sat-Chō navy," but the theory is hardly borne Monopoly. out by the facts. And this applies also to the army. The Sat-Chō clans have a virtual monopoly here, as well as in civil affairs. Satsuma has not only furnished such army leaders as Nogi, Kuroki, and Ōyama, but practically the whole of the navy, from Togo and Yamamoto downward. In the Japanese mind the Satsuma men are credited chiefly with courage, the Chōshū men with sagacity —therefore the former are soldiers and sailors, men of dash and daring, while the latter are diplomatists and chiefs of administration. But the fact is, these two southern clans simply gained control of the government in 1868, and have never relinquished it since—clan-government having supplanted the Shōgunate.

The hero of Port Arthur, Nogi Kiten, is the Japanese ideal of a soldier. His enthu-Nogi, a Typical siastic admirers even call him the Soldier. "incarnation of the imperial war-god." He has given utterance to his own conception of the warrior-life in the following striking language: "When a man becomes a soldier he must be perfectly willing to lead henceforth a life that is somewhat different from the life of an ordinary man. It is impossible for him thereafter to enjoy liberty and wealth in the same manner as his fellows. What I mean is this: that the soldier who would perform his duties with credit on a battle-field must, of necessity, have trained himself to perform all that is expected of him in the days of peace. There ought not to be any neglect or any defects in his daily life. The man who would rightfully aspire to the honor of fighting under the sun-flag must first have learned to be a man through the conquest of himself in times of peace."

That Nogi has practised what he preaches is proved by his memorable words when the news was brought to him that his eldest son —the pride and hope of every Japanese household—had been killed in the battle of Nanshan. "I am glad he died so splendidly," the father said. "It was the greatest honor he could have. As for the funeral rites in his memory, they might as well be postponed for a while. A little later on they may be performed in connection with those to the

memory of my second son, Hoten, and of myself.'' His second son fell during the
Typical
Instances of
Loyalty.
last days of the siege around Port Arthur.

This wondrous spirit of loyalty, inheritance from feudal days, is not confined to the officers of the army, but is shared by the humblest of the people. The Russian war has afforded numberless examples. There was the aged mother, for example, who learned that her soldier-son was detained at home on her account. Slaying herself in patriotic sacrifice, she withdrew the bloody dagger in time to hand it to her son with the Spartan injunction that he should plunge it into the hearts of the enemy. And a story comes of a humble *jinrikisha*-man, who, because he could find no care-taker for his motherless children, slew them and buried them in the family temple grounds, that he might go off to the war. The blanket wherein he wrapped their little dead bodies as he took them to their burial was afterwards cut into shreds by the equally patriotic priest and distributed as priceless relics to the pilgrims who came to do honor at the sacrificial grave. What wonder that Japan wins victories?

And loyalty does more than win battles. It is loyalty in connection with an enlightened clan-government that accounts for the remarkable courtesy of the army. Much as we should like to believe it, doubtless we should err in accounting for the good behavior of the Japanese army altogether' on the grounds of good-nature, or deep-set convictions of mercy. The inherent cruelty of the Japanese soldier is far too thoroughly established, and the barbarous conduct of these same troops on the occasion of the former fall of Port Arthur, only ten years ago, is of much too recent occurrence to allow of such an inner transfiguration of character as would explain on purely moral principles their humane behavior towards the Russians. The true explanation, however, is hardly less wonderful. The clan-government which radiates from the imperial palace in Tōkyō into every regiment of the army and every ship of the navy is one of the most astute bodies of men on earth. They are profoundly watchful of international sentiment in their desire for international regard, and they are also fully familiar with the reverential loyalty of the troops to their Emperor, which they have used every

Loyalty in Lieu of Morals.

means to enhance. Having incurred the opprobrium of the civilized world on account of the Port Arthur massacre, they have forestalled the repetition of such occurrences. How? By an extremely simple expedient, in view of Japanese loyalty. Messages are sent in the name of the Emperor, commanding merciful treatment, and the regard of the troops for their sun-god is such as to serve in the place of a conscience, even amid the carnage of battle, or in spite of temptations to pillage. It will be a serious time of transition when their worship of the Emperor is destroyed.

In accounting for the martial strength of young Japan we must not overlook the com-
Financial mercial astuteness that has made
Development. possible the "sinews of war."
Poor as the Island Empire is, her financiers have made such use of their resources as to produce almost incredible development in an amazingly short space of time. The progress of this financial development is made clear in the following tables: *

---

* For these figures we are chiefly indebted to a little book published in Tōkyō in 1904 by Hoshino Kota, entitled "The Mission of Japan."

A BUSINESS STREET IN MODERN TŌKYŌ.

	1893. Yen.	1903. Yen.
Revenue	44,521,000	146,995,500
Current money	119,229,000	165,576,000
Capital of business firms ..	151,147,000	600,540,000
Capital of banks	55,817,000	263,483,500
Exports	45,074,500	199,751,000
Imports	44,677,500	158,067,500
Import taxes	2,562,500	8,035,500
National debt	141,759,500	280,582,000

During the same period the tonnage value of Japanese steamships grew from 110,000 to 610,000 tons; sailing-vessels, from 45,000 to 334,000 tons; and the naval fleet, from 61,000 to 257,000 tons. The mileage of railways increased from slightly more than 2000 to 5015; and the mileage of electric wires from the neighborhood of 30,000 to more than double that number.

Facts like these made young Japan not only willing, but able, to respond to the call for a war-loan with five times the amount that was needed.

MODERN SCHOOL-DAYS
PART SECOND

IF our study of modern Japanese history has shown us anything at all, it has proved that Book III. of this volume is well named. The fifty years that have passed since Commodore Perry opened the gates of Japan have been for her the busiest "school-days" that any nation has ever experienced. And the people are not yet satisfied. Count Ōkuma, who ranks next to Itō as the greatest living statesman of Japan, is recently reported as saying: "What we need mostly, greatly, is education. Only by education can our people acquire just ideas of their rights and responsibilities under the constitution. Thirty years ago we scarcely knew what education was. Our educational system, although it is not yet equal to that of the United States, Germany, or France, is yet far superior to that of Italy or Spain, or even Australia. Its results are manifest in our army. Our success against China was due, of course, to the personal courage of our soldiers, but it was also, in part, due to the development of our educational system. If they had been as lacking in education as the Chinese mass, our troops would not have been half so successful as they were. When conscription was first adopted [1872], most of our soldiers were illiterate; now many of the annual draft of conscripts are well educated, and almost all of them can read and write. And in the thirty years to come we hope to accomplish much more than we have done in the thirty years past, much as that has been."

What Count Ōkuma has said of the war with China is also true of the more recent struggle with Russia. General Francis V. Greene is authority An Educational Comparison. for the statement that among the conscripts annually drafted by the Russian army, only about three out of a hundred can read and write. "The latest statistics show that in the Russian population of a hundred and forty million only 1,750,000 boys and 550,000 girls were at school, or in all one and a half per cent." On the other hand, out of all the Japanese children of school age, 91.75 per cent. attend schools. In 1903, out of a total population of 46,880,030, there were 4,300,-

000 pupils in elementary schools, eighty thousand in the "middle" schools, six thousand in the "higher" schools, and about four thousand in the various "colleges" at the two universities. These figures take account of the government schools alone, whereas there are numerous private schools and colleges.* It may easily be seen that nearly twelve per cent. of the entire Japanese population are attending school, as against one and a half per cent. in Russia. Does not this fact suggest at least a partial solution of the wonderful successes of the Japanese against the Russians, in spite of the enormous disparity in power? "Knowledge is power."

The Japanese "department of education" was organized by the imperial government in

---

* The statistics for all of the schools of Japan, private as well as governmental, are as follows: 27,154 elementary schools, 19 blind and dumb schools, 57 normal schools, 33 higher normal schools, 5 training schools for teachers, 258 middle schools, 80 higher schools for girls, 8 higher schools or colleges, 2 imperial universities, 58 professional colleges, 853 industrial colleges, 3 training schools for industrial teachers, 1657 miscellaneous institutions. Total, 30,187 schools, with 5,469,410 pupils in attendance.

1871. In that next great year of changes, the Emperor uttered his memorable declaration: "It is intended henceforth Educational that education shall be so diffused Ambition. that there may not be a village with an ignorant family, or a family with an ignorant member." Twenty years later, this wish had been so far fulfilled as to show an increase of more than three million per cent. in the number of Japanese that were acquiring an education. To-day, there is doubtless a slighter proportion of illiteracy in Tōkyō than in cultured Boston.* Japan undertook a task of immeasurable difficulty when the Emperor issued his notable declaration in 1872. "Through languages which she has not mastered she has struggled with ideas which she has not made her own." Despite the poverty, ignorance, and low ideals of the masses, who fail to grasp the significance of knowledge, and notwithstanding the annual shortage of thousands in the teaching force, Japan has persisted in her ambition to cover the whole realm of human investigation and book-learning, until "there shall not be a village with an ignorant family, or a family with an

---

* Mr. Henry Norman, in " The Real Japan."

ignorant member." This vast educational undertaking is only thirty-three years old. "That Japan has not miserably failed, but has succeeded in producing in thirty years a result which Russia, for example, still waits to attempt, marks her as worthy of a great future,"—so writes Mr. R. E. Lewis in "The Educational Conquest of the Far East."* "The young Japanese people, an-hungered of learning, have literally fed upon the erudition of the West until it has begun to grow into their bone and sinew."

The chief educator of modern Japan was without doubt the great Fukuzawa. Becoming Japan's Greatest early convinced of the superiority Educator. of Western learning and civilization, he wrote numerous books that had an immense circulation and an enormous influence in committing Japan to Western ideals. He afterwards founded an

---

* Dr. Albert Shaw carries the comparison further: " Almost two hundred years ago, Peter the Great ordered his subjects to put on Western civilization. Mutsuhito commanded his subjects to do the same one hundred and fifty years later. But, although Russia has had a century and a half the start, Western civilization is still to her an outer garment, while the Japanese have made it a part of their national life."

extensive private college, with a large faculty and a thousand students. Professor Chamberlain says that "this eminent private schoolmaster, who might be minister of education, but who has consistently refused all office, is the intellectual father of half the young men who now fill the middle and lower posts in the government of Japan." This is the more significant when we remember that from the beginning he steadfastly combated the ancient ideals of Japan, such as suicide, often at the peril of his life. While not a professing Christian, we are informed that "at the opening of the twentieth century, being even more pro-Christian, he was vigorously opposed by reactionaries as the preacher of 'Occidental,' that is, Christian morals. Hosts of his friends on either side of the Pacific rejoiced in the recognition of his work for the good of his countrymen in the gift from the Emperor in connection with the crown prince's wedding, in May, 1900, of fifty thousand *yen*, in lieu of a patent of nobility, which would have been gladly conferred, only that Fukuzawa preferred to remain a commoner." He died two years later. In addition to his work as an author, he was a distinguished and influ-

19

ential journalist.   His best known work is
the " Promotion of Learning," in seventeen
volumes, which has had a Japanese sale of
two hundred thousand complete sets.

It may now be worth while to present a
brief view of the present system of govern-
The   mental education, beginning with
Educational   the university, which is the hub of
System.   the educational wheel.   A second
university has been recently established at
Kyōto, but, as it is still in its primary stages,
we need consider only the great university at
Tōkyō. We have already seen that Verbeck
became its first director in the year 1869,
although it was not formally organized until
several years later. At present it consists of
a university hall, six colleges, two hospitals,
The   astronomical and seismological ob-
University.   servatories, a botanical garden, a
marine biological station, several museums
and laboratories, and a library of 330,000
volumes, of which almost one-half are in English and other foreign tongues. The educational tendencies of Japan may be measured
by the fact that when the Emperor decreed
a hundred and twenty-three professorships
for the university in 1893, he specified that
they should be in the following proportion:

twenty-three in medicine, twenty-two in law, twenty-one in engineering, twenty in literature and in agriculture, with seventeen in science. The catalogue for the session of 1901–1902 shows that there were 3213 students in attendance, and that thirty-one assistant professors were studying abroad. The subjects pursued by the absent instructors embraced agriculture, architecture, chemistry, surgery, dentistry, pharmacy, clinical bacteriology, veterinary medicine and hygiene, comparative legal institutions, the science of religion, diplomatic history, forest utilization, iron metallurgy, and statistics. The Japanese exhibit at the St. Louis Fair contained two interesting scientific inventions by professors in this university. The first was an apparatus for measuring the variation in length of a magnetized body by means of magnetization—so that measurements may be had, under conditions obtained by optical arrangement, having an accuracy of five-millionths of a centimetre. The other invention is called a tromometer, an improvement upon the seismometer for the measurements of earthquakes. Since the invention of this instrument, it has become possible to predict Japanese earthquakes twenty-four hours in advance of their coming!

It will be noted that especial attention is given to the study of medicine, with its col-

Proficiency in Medicine. lateral branches. Indeed, the appropriation for the College of Medicine is three times greater than for any of the other colleges. This is in harmony with the fact that the Japanese have a singular genius for medicine and surgery. They pay far more critical attention to medical training than we do here in America. At a time when no medical school in this country demanded more than three years for graduation, the Japanese required, after the conclusion of a four years' course (of ten months each), an examination that covered twenty-four days, wherein each candidate was compelled to diagnose and treat from day to day several cases in the university hospitals. After an experience of five years with physicians in various parts of the empire, I have no hesitation in saying that the modern Japanese practitioner is even more capable than our own, and that this superiority holds good to a still greater extent when the comparison extends to the hospitals.

But we may comfort ourselves, perhaps, in

the matter of music. Commodore Perry's narrative tersely informs us that "little can be said in commendation of their music." Miss Bacon, in " Japanese Girls and Women," demurely observes: "It seems to me quite fortunate that the musical art is not more generally practised;" whereupon Professor Chamberlain remarks, "That is what every one thinks, though most Europeans of the stronger sex would use considerably stronger expressions to relieve their feelings on the matter." The very latest essayist on Japan, Mr. Watson, positively avows: "There is no music indigenous to Japan, nor are there native musical instruments. This I affirm in the full knowledge that there is a Japanese scale of five notes, and that there are instruments named *samisen* and *koto*. I repeat, there is no music indigenous to Japan, nor are there musical instruments native to the country."

The so-called "musical instruments" of Japan are chiefly the *samisen*, the *koto*, the *kokyū*, and the *biwa*. The *samisen* is the most popular instrument, being in the hands of every tea-house girl and love-lorn swain. It is a mongrel three-stringed banjo, imported from Manila in

1700. The *koto* is a kind of zither, or dulcimer, with thirteen strings, and is a favorite with the better classes of the people. It is a long, narrow, wooden affair, which is laid flat upon the floor, and manipulated after the fashion of a mandolin. Its tones are much more pleasing than the *samisen* (than which nothing could be worse), but it is correspondingly difficult to play. It is an evolution from a Chinese model, and was perfected in the seventeenth century by Yatsuhashi, who is called the father of modern Japanese music. The *kokyū* is a fiddle of three strings, and the less said about it the better. The *biwa* is a large, pear-shaped, four-string lute, commonly played by old people. It was once the writer's privilege to attend a classical concert in Tōykō. He never went again. The musicians sat around on the floor of the stage, while the audience waited in reverential silence. Presently the silence was broken by a wild welter of sound that soon drove me, in the effort to retain my dignity, almost to the point of distraction. To make matters worse, each of the solemn performers would occasionally open his or her mouth and emit a most astonishing howl, compounded of profound canine sorrow and the nasal honk of a wild goose. There is a curious Shintō ceremony known as a silent concert. Various instruments are employed, but "it is held that the sanctity of the occasion would be profaned were any sound to fall on profane ears. Therefore, though all the motions of playing are gone through, no strains are actually emitted." This is the most truly musical concert which the native art has evolved.

The Japanese scale is a matter of dispute. It is sometimes understood to consist of five notes of the harmonic minor scale, the fourth and seventh being omitted, but different opinions are advanced by differing scholars. Indeed, a thoughtful article on "The Music of Japan" in the *Japan Mail* declares that "no one has learned enough about Japanese music to warrant him in determining the key of a single tune." This same essay asserts that the final verdict of experts regarding Japanese music will be somewhat as follows: "Music in this country came into existence in obedience to a natural inspiration, precisely as it did elsewhere. Its growth, to a certain point, was regulated by the same principles as those under which the melodies of the Greeks were gradually developed. These

melodies passed through the early centuries
of the Christian era, and prevailed in Europe
until many of their forms were found incom-
patible with the great system of which the
Benedictines of Florence were the first ex-
ponents—though probably not the inventors.
Then the Greek music was re-created. But
the music of Japan has never been re-created.
It is of similar grade to that which was, for
the most part, rejected by the mediæval har-
monists, as having no proper standing in
progressive art. It happened, however, that
among the modes derived from the Greeks
some were found which yielded readily to the
new science, and upon these the forms of modern melody were doubtless based. We are
not aware that any corresponding forms
have been discovered in Japanese music. All
the examples that we have had the opportunity of examining appear to represent
modes which reached their limit ages ago.—
In a word, Japanese music, as we have it
handed down by tradition, belongs to the
past, and has no affinity with the European
music of to-day. There is nothing in it that
can be further developed while allowing it to
retain its national character.'' It may be
added that there is an extremely complicated

notation for "classical" music, but none for the more popular forms.

The high-grade or classical tools of music embrace a variety of wind- and stringed-in-struments imported ages ago from Music and India by way of China. Music, like Esotericism. poetry and porcelain-making in Japan, has always been more or less esoteric in charac-ter. Esotericism, indeed, has been affected by artists and artisans of every art and craft throughout the ages—even to such prosaic pursuits as bone-setting and cookery, to say nothing of fencing and *jiū-jutsu*. To-day every town has its *mei-butsu*, or "famous product," to be had nowhere else, because fostered by some local family in secret the ages through. A pretty story illustrative of the esoteric in music comes down to us from the tenth century. At that time there lived a great musician, Hakuga, whose contempo-rary, Semi-Maro, was a greater musician still. This past-master of his art lived in absolute seclusion, with no companion but his lute, and there was a melody whereof he alone possessed the secret. "Hakuga went every evening for three years to listen sur-reptitiously at Semi's gate, but all in vain. Finally, one autumn night, when the wind

was soughing through the sedges, and the
moon was half-hidden by a cloud, Hakuga's
ravished ears were blessed with the secret
magic strains—and when they ceased, he
heard the master exclaim, 'Alas, that there
should be no one to whom I might transmit
my precious secret!' Emboldened by this
remark, Hakuga entered the hermitage, pros-
trated himself, and humbly implored to be
received as Semi's disciple. His prayer was
granted, and Semi gradually revealed to him
all of the innermost recesses of his esoteric
art." It must be borne in mind, however,
that the strains which ravished Japanese ears
would probably have set a European's teeth
on edge—such are the prosaic facts in the
case. Nevertheless, while the Japanese are
sadly deficient in the development of native
music, they have proved themselves meas-
urably able pupils of the Western school.
The writer used to go on Saturday even-
ings with great enjoyment to the services of
the Greek Cathedral in Tōkyō, where Bishop
Nicolai and his associates had trained a noble
chorus to intone the ancient Christian chants.
Dr. Ladd, of Yale, went so far as to say in
my hearing that this was the noblest chorus
singing he had ever heard. And Mr. Wat-

son, who has already been quoted in condemnation of the native music, pays an eloquent and appreciative tribute to the proficiency of a "westernized" orchestra in Tōkyō. The fact remains, however, that music is the science in which the Japanese have made least progress during their Occidental school-days, while medicine is at the other extreme.

Let us return from this diversion to a further examination of the system of government schools. Next to the imperial university come the *Higher Schools.* "higher schools," corresponding very nearly to the average American college. These are eight in number, and are situated in various parts of the empire. They are almost invariably fitting schools for the university, as no student proceeds thus far unless bent on professional pursuits. About six thousand students are enrolled in these "higher schools," and an average of fifty teachers to a single institution. "No degrees are given, and the fees vary according to the courses followed." The course usually covers four years.

In an ever widening circle from the great university at the centre, the system now branches out into the "middle schools," corresponding to our academies and high

Middle Schools. schools, of which there are two hundred and fifty-eight under the direction of government, with an enrolment of nearly eighty thousand. While the government directs these institutions, they are usually supported by the various prefectures. The course of study covers five years. It is arranged to serve the purpose of preparing either for the "higher schools," or for the practical pursuits of common life. English is the most important study, with Japanese and Chinese ranking next. Athletics is accorded great attention, owing to the desire of the people for a better physique. Mathematics and history are treated as of much importance, while ethics receives scant consideration. The course further includes a second foreign language, with geography, natural sciences, writing, drawing, and a little singing.

As already mentioned, there are 4,300,000 pupils in the "elementary" schools of Japan, Elementary Schools. of which there are about twenty-seven thousand. The government states that these schools, which are in two grades, are "designed to give children the rudiments of moral education, and of education especially adapted to make of them good members of the community, together with such general knowledge and skill as are necessary for practical life, due attention being paid to their physical development.'' The course of study varies from two to four years. Every village is required to have an elementary school, and each child that has reached the age of six years is compelled to take at least four years of public schooling. The elementary institutions are supported either by the community or by individuals. So vital is the concern for education that in 1896 the voluntary contributions for the support of schools had already reached the sum of 750,000 *yen* ($375,000). This was in addition to several thousand acres of land, with books and school apparatus, besides the large educational taxes. The elementary schools include industrial features, such as simple farming for the boys and sewing for their sisters. Kindergartens are here and there provided, especially in the largest of the cities. ''In certain points they are still open to improvement, but in their buildings, their rules regulating space, air, and other hygienic matters, the kindergartens of the

West might go to school to Japan." This brings us to the bottom of the educational ladder provided by the government.

But it must not be overlooked that for the purpose of furnishing teachers for the ele-
Normal Schools, mentary schools, the government
etc. supports more than fifty normal schools, which accomplish a most effective work. There are also various technical colleges that have reached a high grade of efficiency. The curriculum of the Tōkyō Higher Technical School includes mechanical engineering, electro-chemistry, applied chemistry, dyeing, weaving, ceramics, designing, and making of cuts for printing. The most seriously neglected class of students is the women, as might naturally be expected of a country so lately unbound from the degrading teachings of Confucius. Even in the normal schools the men are largely preponderant. The government has taken
Female a higher stand for the education of
Education. women since the year 1890, when the educational minister declared in his official report that "female education is the source from which general education should be diffused over the whole country." There were then only eight government

A PRIMARY SCHOOL FOR GIRLS.

schools for women, with an attendance of three thousand. Ten years later, there were forty-four such schools, with an attendance of almost twelve thousand. "The course of study extends over five years, with twenty-five hours of prescribed work each week, including, however, such relaxing subjects as household management, singing, and gymnastics." But it is difficult to make the people see the importance of the education of girls. There is an independent university for women in Tōkyō, established a few years ago, which marks another new era in the education of the Japanese women.

There is one radical and alarming defect in the entire system of government schools: the moral and religious element is almost totally ignored. This is in accord with the well-known views of Marquis Itō, who seems to dominate modern Japan. "I myself look to science, knowledge, culture, as a sufficient religion,"— that is his uttered creed. At times the attitude of the educational department has become so antagonistic to Christianity as to threaten the violation of the constitution, which declares that "Japanese subjects shall, within limits not prejudicial to

The Radical Flaw.

peace and order, and not antagonistic to
their duties as subjects, enjoy freedom of
religious belief.'' In 1899–1900, the minister
for education issued an order directly hostile
to the numerous Christian schools, and the
vice-minister declared that ''while the constitution allows liberty to believe any religion,
yet this does not necessarily mean liberty
to propagate it!'' The Diet has since then
passed an ordinance that makes it impossible
for discriminations to be made against Christianity; but this does not alter the fact that
the government educational system is conducted on thoroughly irreligious principles.
Its attitude is accurately expressed in the
recent utterance of a university professor:
''We shall go to China—in fact, we are
already there—with a harmonious blending
of the best precepts in Buddhism, Confucianism, Bushidō, Brahmanism, Herbert Spencer,
Christianity, and other systems of thought,
and we shall, I think, have little trouble in
awakening the naturally agnostic mind of the
Chinese to the enlightenment of modern free
thought. . . . We confidently believe that it
has been assigned to Japan to lead the world
in this new intellectual era in the progress of
mankind.''

There are two features of this characteristic declaration that invite the most serious attention. In the first place, it cannot be questioned that Japan *The problem.* is sooner or later to become the schoolmaster of China, and China holds a third of the human race. In the second place, the new gospel which Japan proposes to champion has proved sadly insufficient for her own needs. For, in spite of her advance in education, there has been actual retrogression in morals. Count Kabayama, the very minister who antagonized Christianity, confessed that the young men of Japan are now on a lower moral plane than were the young men of the preceding generation. And the successor of the great Fukuzawa as president of the largest private college in the empire recently declared in a public address: "It looks as though corruption covered every part of public works and education, so that children in leaving their homes to go to school must tramp over roads constructed by bribery, must cross bridges built by bribery, must enter school buildings erected by bribery, and while reading the educational text-books their teachers are arrested for bribery!" This was in allusion to a great scandal that

20

makes the year 1903 notorious in the educational history of Japan,—when it was discovered that the system to which had been entrusted the moral education of the Japanese youth was honeycombed with rottenness from end to end.   Japan is the only nation that has ever dared to separate religion wholly from government, and morals from law,—to make reason a sole and sufficient guide,—and Japan is paying the penalty. Shall Japan be allowed to substitute moral suicide for her ancient code of *hara-kiri,* and to diffuse the poison of religious indifference throughout Asia?

In a previous section of this book attention was directed to five noble qualities of Japanese character: bravery, loyalty, alertness, thoroughness, and self-control. To the superficial, this might seem to be a sufficient moral equipment for any nation. But a little thought convinces otherwise. What is bravery worth without purity? What value has loyalty without honesty? The intellect must not only be alert and thorough, but it must also be sincere. The will must learn not only self-control, it must also learn self-reverence. The two cancers at the core of the Japanese character are deep-set dis-

Japanese Morals.

honesty and abandoned impurity; either would be sufficient to wreck the life of any nation.

Let it not be said that this is the prejudiced opinion of an unsympathetic outsider.   A Japanese journalist recently confessed that "our countrymen have earned an unenviable reputation of being the most untrustworthy people on earth," and admitted that they had earned it justly. As for the other, Japan is the only civilized government that deals in licensed prostitution as a source of revenue, and tolerates the sale of young girls by their parents under guise of a regard for "filial piety."

Christianity has had considerable influence in widening the moral conceptions of the people, and in deepening these into subsequent convictions. The pervasiveness of this influence has already been distinctly suggested in connection with the career of Verbeck; nor must such institutions as the Red Cross Society be left out of account. Besides, the presence throughout the empire of scores of mission schools is having a profound educational effect. As to the actual number of converts, this propaganda is not yet fifty years old, but has nevertheless gained an average annual following of almost a thousand members, while the number of annual accessions for several years past has been three thousand or more. And the membership has been recruited from among the most influential classes—including members of parliament, legislators, judges, officers in the army and navy, lawyers, bankers, physicians, and editors.

But the stubborn fact remains that for every inhabitant of Japan who is influenced by Christian standards of conduct, there are 999 whose highest ideals centre in devotion to the Emperor, and have no radius whatsoever. We must not permit the glamour of their splendid patriotism to blind us to the unpleasant fact that the Japanese as a people are not even the ethical equals of their backward neighbors in China. In spite of its infinite charm, Japan is still a country where the word "lie" has no unpleasant associations whatever; being not a term of reproach, but rather implying a jocular compliment. The commercial dishonesty of Japanese merchants has become a byword among the nations, and is a serious hindrance to Oriental trade—in striking contrast with China. Duplicity of the most repulsive character is often masked by the curious "Japanese smile." An offensive, even nauseating, conceit often mars the grace of the popular manners. Japanese social impurity is as much of a national byword as commercial dishonesty; the *Yoshiwara* quarter in every town and city being not only a licensed institution, but invariably the best-built and most prosperous section of the municipality. And yet, in spite of a wofully decadent morality, material and even intellectual progress goes forward by leaps and bounds. It is this enormous disparity between material and moral advancement that makes the future of Japan so problematical. It is the evolution of a real world-power that we have witnessed; but whether this power shall prove a curse or a blessing to mankind will depend upon the nature of the further educational training of "Young Japan."

The sanest of her leaders perceive the importance of this fact most clearly. We are told that an important member of the Japanese judiciary recently expressed himself as follows: "From a purely materialistic point of view the Japanese have absorbed more or less all European civilization, but at the same time the process has

The Future?

been only superficial, and it cannot truthfully
be said that the nation as a whole has absorbed it, or that they are civilized from a
European point of view. There is a void
somewhere; that void will have to be supplied by the idealism of the West, which has
been entirely ignored by Japan, while the
materialism has been successfully assimi-
lated.—It therefore seems to me that if we
take in the material civilization of Europe we
must also take in to counterbalance it the
idealism and spiritual soul, as it were, of
Occidental enlightenment. The course of tui-
tion will take place gradually. The merchants, if they persist in their present prac-
tices, will inevitably lose their clients, and it
will then begin to dawn upon them that they
must be honest and thoroughly upright in
order to succeed in life in the proper sense of
the term.''

Count Ōkuma, who ranks next to Itō as the
most able of Japanese statesmen, acknowl-
edges the same disease and suggests the same
remedy, only with the use of plainer language. Repudiating the purely cultural
creed of his great associate,* albeit not him-

* See page 303.

self a follower of the Christian faith, Count Ōkuma has recently issued the following striking statement: "It is a question whether as a people we have not lost fibre as a result of the many new influences to which we have been subjected.—Development has been intellectual and not moral. The efforts that Christians are making to supply to the country a high standard of conduct are welcomed by all right-thinking people. As one reads the Bible one may think it antiquated, out of date. The words it contains may so appear, but the noble life that it holds up to admiration is something that will never be out of date, however much the world may progress. Live and preach this life, and you will supply to the nation just what it needs at the present crisis."

The present *is* a crisis in the life of this sturdy young nation. Shall Ōkuma's advice prevail, or Itō's? Upon the answer to this question depends the future manhood of Japan.

INDEX

JAPAN TO-DAY

By JAMES A. B. SCHERER, PH.D.

With 28 illustrations (two in colors) from photographs and
prints by native artists. 12mo. Decorated cloth,
$1.50, net.

"An exceedingly well-written, bright, and timely book, worth
careful consideration, as it is more than a traveller's tale of strange
scenes and people."—*The Philadelphia Evening Telegraph*.

"Dr. Scherer's observations on the social life of the Japanese, and
especially on their system of modern education, are as valuable as
they are bright and optimistic."—*The Brooklyn Daily Eagle*.

"Full of the most delightful humor. We are grateful to Dr.
Scherer for adding materially to the knowledge of those who are
dependent upon others for first-hand impressions of the Japanese."—
Providence Journal.

"Gives the clearest, most rational explanation of the Japanese as
they are, of any book that we have read."—*Buffalo Commercial*.

PRESENT-DAY JAPAN

By AUGUSTA M. CAMPBELL DAVIDSON, M.A.

Colored frontispiece and 73 illustrations. Decorated cloth,
$4.50, net.

"The materials for this book were gathered in the course of a
lengthy visit to Japan, during which the author associated chiefly with
Japanese, and enjoyed exceptional opportunities of observing present
social conditions. The book is written in a bright and picturesque
style, and records with the vividness natural to freshly-received impressions the writer's own experiences of travel and intercourse with
the natives. It contains descriptions of town and country customs,
sketches of present-day life and character in Tokyo and elsewhere, of
the scenery of famous places, with their legends and associations, of
the drama of the nation, and of its religious creeds, etc. ; and is profusely illustrated by photographs and drawings made by the author.

J. B. LIPPINCOTT COMPANY, PHILADELPHIA.

HISTORY OF THE MOORISH EMPIRE IN EUROPE

By S. P. SCOTT

3 volumes. Royal 8vo. Decorated cloth, gilt tops, rough edges, $10.00 per set.

A scholarly and comprehensive review of one of the most interesting and influential periods in European history. Mr. Scott lived for some time in Spain, and he has approached his subject with the deliberation and exhaustive study which give his discussion the poise and coherence that are the attributes only of the most distinguished of historical writing. The examination of original manuscripts and other material occupied the author for twenty years ; and the work depicts the civilization of a race whose achievements in science, literature, and the arts were an inspiration.

"With its tremendous list of authorities in many languages, its all-inclusive conception of the province of history, his work has the crowning advantage of being ever vivid, and therefore unflaggingly interesting."—*Mail and Express.*

"There is no other work covering the period of Moorish dominion in Europe in anything approaching an adequate manner—certainly nothing in English which makes a pretense at completeness."—*The New York Globe.*

"With a rare gift in the selection of the chapters of history which are most filled with 'human interest,' Mr. Scott has also a peculiar charm of style—a certain keenness which has served to make the events of a distant past fascinating. The history of the Moorish people in Europe, as he presents it, is infinitely more absorbing and ever exciting than any chapter of fiction ever written."—*The San Francisco Bulletin.*

J. B. LIPPINCOTT COMPANY, PHILADELPHIA.

TEUTONIC LEGENDS IN THE NIBE-LUNGEN LIED AND THE NIBELUNGEN RING

By W. C. SAWYER, Ph.D. With an Introductory Essay
By Prof. F. SCHULTZE, Ph.D.

Illustrated. Decorated cloth, $2.00, net.

"To every student of operatic music as well as to all opera goers who possess appreciation of the significance of music in its higher forms, this volume by the Professor of the German Language and Teutonic Mythology in the University of the Pacific will appeal with especial force. It is, as its title indicates, a presentation of the legends which underlie the Nibelungen Lied and the Nibelungen Ring, and it is free from the oppression of an excess of technical terms.

"One of the most interesting as well as the latest is a well-made volume on 'Teutonic Legends.' A good index completes this important contribution to Wagnerian literature."—*Cleveland Plain-Dealer*.

"Those who have become more or less familiar with the 'Nibelungen Ring' but have not access to German literature in the original, may learn much of the sources of the work and of its relation to the whole body of Teutonic legends, in the very attractive volume prepared by Dr. Sawyer."—*Philadelphia Public Ledger*.

J. B. LIPPINCOTT COMPANY, PHILADELPHIA.

The True History of the American Revolution.

By SYDNEY GEORGE FISHER.

These are the real facts of the days of 1776. Mr. Fisher has some things to tell about the conduct of the War of the Revolution, its chief figures, and the reasons for its outcome, which will startle every reader of American history.

He writes of the smuggling, rioting, and revolt against control which marked the exercise of the Taxing Acts ; the Tea Party in Boston ; the Reign of Terror ; Howe, the Political General ; Whigery and Weakness ; the Pretended Loyalty of the Colonists ; the Price of Bunker Hill ; ''the Best Campaign of the War ;'' the Battles about Boston, Philadelphia, and on Long Island ; the Abandonment of Burgoyne ; the Campaign in the South ; the Hopeless Year of 1780 ; and of Yorktown.

Twenty-four illustrations. Crown 8vo. Cloth, decorated, $2.00, *net*. Postage, 14 cents extra.

J. B. LIPPINCOTT COMPANY, PHILADELPHIA.

BUSINESS

By L. deV. MATTHEWMAN

———

Profusely illustrated. 12mo.
Decorated cloth, $1.00, net.

———

A series of snappy epigrams by the author of "Crankisms," on the principles and lack of principles in business.

It is full of humorous philosophy on practical men and things in tablet form. Fifty full-page and many smaller sketches by Tom Fleming.

> "Spiced with the cleverness necessary to the success of all smartness, these aphorisms are both witty and wise."— *Toledo Blade*, Ohio.

———

J. B. LIPPINCOTT COMPANY, PHILADELPHIA

DISEASES OF SOCIETY

By G. FRANK LYDSTON, M.D.

———

*8vo.   Illustrated.   Cloth, $3.00, net.
Postage, 17 cents extra.*

———

An outspoken study of phases of the vice and crime problem and social conditions before untouched on in a work of general circulation.

Dr. Lydston fearlessly discusses the criminal, anarchist, sexual pervert, and the vast number of offenders against the moral law in society at large whom the courts do not reach.   The author takes up the oppression of wealth, the rights and wrongs of organized capital and labor, the negro question and the crimes which have grown out of it.   Dr. Lydston has had unusual opportunities in the study of these subjects, including access to police records, and the private and public photograph galleries of many cities.

The work is liberally illustrated from many special photographs.

———

J. B. LIPPINCOTT COMPANY, PHILADELPHIA